Artificial Intelligence and Machine Learning for Business for Non-Engineers

Artificial Intelligence and Machine Learning for Business for Non-Engineers

Edited by
Frank M. Groom and Stephan S. Jones

CRC Press
Taylor & Francis Group
Boca Raton London New York

CRC Press is an imprint of the
Taylor & Francis Group, an **informa** business

CRC Press
Taylor & Francis Group
6000 Broken Sound Parkway NW, Suite 300
Boca Raton, FL 33487-2742

© 2020 by Taylor & Francis Group, LLC
CRC Press is an imprint of Taylor & Francis Group, an Informa business

No claim to original U.S. Government works

Printed on acid-free paper

International Standard Book Number-13: 978-0-367-36574-5 (Paperback)

Visit the Taylor & Francis Web site at
http://www.taylorandfrancis.com

and the CRC Press Web site at
http://www.crcpress.com

Contents

Preface

Technology and machinery have been ever-changing subjects since the first shavings were taken off of a rock to create a sharp-enough tool to kill and skin primitive food supplies. This eventually paved the way for simple machines and technology to ease the daily lives of everyone – with each new advance impacting the way work was done previously. Fast forward to the future and technology is now capable of processing massive amounts of data in a split second, analyzing billions of bits of information to tug out the digital needle in a haystack. All of this leads the world into a new realm that seems to be on the tip of every company and innovator's spear as they gear up to attack a new economy: artificial intelligence and learning machines.

This book will serve as an introduction to the field and technology that make up artificial intelligence and learning machines (AI and LM). It will delve deeper into specific fields that are optimized by the use and integration of AI and LM into their daily used systems in a non-technical manner to allow for the reader to gain knowledge of the emerging systems without the need to learn the algorithms. Some of these fields will include security, marketing, education, healthcare, IT management, and medical devices. This book will also inform individuals without an academic background in technology further insight into the often-daunting world of artificial intelligence. Knowledge gained in this book will support a knowledge base when discussing the world of AI and LM and help decision makers understand the critical components of the technologies. Further knowledge will be required to explore and achieve a greater breadth of understanding in the world of AI and LM; these tools will need to be part of everyone's lexicon in the near future as they will be part of every new technology.

Acknowledgment

The authors would like to thank Derick Brady and Skylar McArthur for their management, research, and patience in putting this edited book together. Without their help, this book would not have been possible.

Editors

Frank M. Groom is a Professor of Information and Communication Sciences at the Center for Information and Communication Sciences at Ball State University. He has conducted research into high-bandwidth networking and the storage and transmission of multimedia objects. He has most recently concentrated his research into Multi-Protocol Label Switching (MPLS)-driven fiber networks, intelligent agents, network-based data deployment, cloud computing, big data storage and analysis, network security, and artificial intelligence and machine learning. Most recently, he has delivered a network and data security class and his 2016 textbook of the same name as well as an Artificial Intelligence and Machine Learning class. Both have been filmed for online delivery. He has conducted a number of national research projects using surveys, focus groups, personal interviews, and student research culminating in two of his earlier published books. Furthermore, he has conducted many specialized statistical research studies for AT&T, McDonalds Corp., and Nth Dimension Software.

Furthermore, Dr. Groom annually conducts a graduate Research Methods course for Ball State graduate students where he teaches many of the methods he has employed in his own research conducted both in industry and at the university level studying both big data problems as well as smaller situations.

Dr. Groom is currently examining the detailed infrastructure and operations of Cloud Data Centers. He is visiting a number of such centers, examining the process by which they distribute processing and storage across racks and arrays of inexpensive components. He furthermore is investigating the approaches Cloud Centers take to elevate control and operations to minimally managed control centers by means of software-defined approaches. He is now extending that investigation into how carriers such as AT&T and Verizon are transforming the control and components of their national networks as software-defined structures with provisioning of virtual network slices of services from customers, similar to the cloud computing approach.

Dr. Groom has presented networking and data processing courses to major American corporations, among whom are PricewaterhouseCoopers; IBM; AT&T and its various units including Bell Labs; Motorola; Digital Equipment Corp. (now HP); Unisys; Ford Motor; Hillenbrand Industries; and McDonalds. IBM sponsored him to present courses on chip engineering and wireless networking to Motorola's engineering teams in Hong Kong and Macao in 1993. AT&T has twice sponsored him to present advanced data processing and networking courses to the graduate students and faculty of Beijing University of Posts and Telecommunications (BUPT) and the People's Republic of China Government Office of Telecommunications. He was honored with being the plenary speaker and having two of his papers presented at the Plenary Session of the 1996 International Conference on Information Infrastructure (ICII'96) in Beijing, China, and a paper presented as the Plenary Session for the World Broadband 2000 conference in Tokyo. Furthermore, in 1996, 1998, and 2006, he presented papers on ATM networking, multimedia, and VoIP at the leading French Graduate School of Telecommunications (Ecole Nationale Superiore des Telecommunications – ENST). In addition to publishing over 120 technical papers concerning networking, systems design, corporate re-engineering, and object-oriented storage, he has published 12 books and contributed chapters in many other books.

Dr. Groom has a Ph.D. in Management Information Systems from the University of Wisconsin-Milwaukee, all but dissertation (ABD) in Statistics from NYU, MBA from the University of Hartford, and AB in Mathematics from the College of the Holy Cross. He was Division Manager in charge of the Information Systems and Data Processing Division of Wisconsin Bell and is the retired Senior Director of Information Systems for Ameritech (now once again part of AT&T).

Stephan S. Jones joined the Center for Information and Communication Sciences faculty in August 1998. He came to Ball State University (BSU) from completing his doctoral studies at Bowling Green State University where he served as the Dean of Continuing Education, developing a distance-learning program for the College of Technology's undergraduate Technology Education program. He was instrumental in bringing the new program on board because of his technical background and extensive research in the distance-learning field.

Prior to coming to higher education, Dr. Jones spent over sixteen and a half years in the communication technology industry. He owned his own teleconnect, providing high-end commercial voice and data networks to a broad range of end users. He provided all the engineering and technical support for his organization that grew to over twenty employees and two and a half million dollars per year revenue. Selling his portion of the organization in December 1994, he worked briefly for Panasonic Communications and Systems Company as a District Sales Manager providing application engineering and product support to distributors in a five-state area prior to starting doctoral studies.

Since coming to BSU, Dr. Jones has been engaged in development efforts to provide up-to-date research opportunities outside of the classroom on areas associated with broadband delivery systems, unified communications, healthcare information technologies, cloud infrastructure, and cybersecurity, and has appeared as a presenter at international, national, and regional technical and economic development gatherings. He has been the Co-Director of the Center's Applied Research Institute, Director of the Australia Centre, and actively involved in the University's community. He has written/edited eighteen books, authored numerous book chapters, and presented at conferences and seminars delivering content related to simplifying the complexity of information and communication technologies. He served ten years as the Director of the largest graduate STEM program at Ball State University, being charged with external funding development, student career development and placement, pursuit of new curriculum ideas, graduate student recruiting, and the out-of-classroom learning experience of the Student Social Learning Program.

Contributors

Joe Ciuffo
Product Marketing
Genesys
San Francisco, California

Lauren Donahue
Solution Architect
Lev+
Indianapolis, Indiana

Sophie Guetzko
Infrastructure Consultant
Accenture
Chicago, Illinois

Fatemeh Hajizadeh
Solution Architect
Lev+
Indianapolis, Indiana

Annie Jay
Healthcare Consulting Practice
Impact Advisors
Naperville, Illinois

Laura Lauer
Healthcare Consulting Practice
Impact Advisors
Naperville, Illinois

Matthew Lievertz
Software Development
Zylo
Indianapolis, Indiana

Kasia Majowski
Healthcare Consulting Practice
Impact Advisors
Naperville, Illinois

Dushyanth Maratt
Sales
ITC Infotech
Ellicott City, Maryland

Rashida Peete
Healthcare Consulting Practice
Impact Advisors
Naperville, Illinois

Dave Pickens
Infrastructure and Architecture
    Analysis
Pace Harmon
Indianapolis, Indiana

Ryan Suter
Business Analyst
enVista
Carmel, Indiana

Chapter 1

Introduction to Artificial Intelligence and Machine Learning

Frank M. Groom

Ball State University

Contents

As the promise of Artificial Intelligence (AI) becomes the hot topic of the information technology world, Silicon Valley companies are allocating sizable resources toward developing and trialing their various products. Meanwhile giants such as Google are buying up promising AI companies such as AlphaGo which was created by the London-based company, DeepMind. AlphaGo then proceeded to beat the Go world champion Ke Jie (Russell, 2017)". Meanwhile Ford, Tesla, and others are in the late development process of producing an automobile that drives itself.

These newsworthy incidents have heightened the interest of technocrats while simultaneously alerting the doomsayers. Apparently both are correct. AI and its partner, Machine Learning, are holding out enormous potential in all areas of business, communication, health, transportation, warehousing and delivery, on-line wholesale and retail, manufacturing, assembly, military, and even the last bastion government services. The benefits of automated decision-making and precision handling of objects have been gradually altering many areas of business from Amazon's Fulfillment Centers to Mercedes, BMW, and Tesla's virtually completely automated car assembly factories (McKinsey, 2017, 2018).

Although many believe there are limits to where AI can penetrate business operations, it increasingly appears that no job is safe from automation assistance and in some cases complete replacement (Bomey, 2017). In the 1990s, American businesses began the move of assembly and manufacturing work to the countries of Southeast Asia where labor rates were no more than 1%–3% of American rates, and as Labor Unions lost power, jobs were moved to the US Southern states and then on to Mexico and Southeast Asia. However, labor rates in those new assembly and manufacturing countries quickly began their own rise. Now China seeks to be the dominant player in offering Artificial Intelligent products to the world and is beginning to install such software in their own factories.

Initially it was thought that only the routine daily repetitive activities of white-collar work could be automated. But now with the demonstrated decision-making capabilities of IBM's Deep Blue and Watson, and Google's AlphaGo, there is no reason to expect decision-making jobs are the exception. Even the areas that seemed impenetrable, such as writing and journalism, are being invaded. As *The New York Times* has noted, AI programs are widely being employed to sift through millions of items for financial news postings daily and summarizing them and even subsequently writing standard articles for direct posting to various news outlets and newspapers.

So where will the new jobs arise. Obviously the initial expectation is that there will be a dramatic demand for program coders, particularly those with the interest, intelligence, and coding skill to address AI and the enhancement of its capabilities by Machine Learning. The training of Machine Learning through thousands of actual examples augmented by continued learning from the Machine Learning Module's actual live experiences has appealed to many potential programming hopefuls. Particularly attracted are the many game players and those who have devoted themselves to writing, sharing, and publishing their own games or variations on existing games. And the plentiful number of coding workshops, coding camps, and self-help on-line tutorials have set the stage for additional numbers who have interest to enter the programming community. Some will join the high-tech development community; some will become entrepreneurs and develop their own AI products. Others will join the business community as purchasers, analysts, implements, testers, and systems managers of the AI product line (Berbazzani, 2018).

However, there will be some limitations. With the emergence of Microsoft's DeepCoder which searches through stacks of programmed routines and assembles programs from these libraries of code, Matej Balog at the University of Cambridge, along with Microsoft Research's Alexander L. Gaunt, Marc Brockschmidt, Sebastian Nowozin, and Daniel Tarlow, has begun the inevitable process of building AI coding programs that are tasked with assembling and writing, and required code on demand without the assistance of human coders.

Others say that human communication is the great barrier, but increasingly the initial experiments with automated help desks and other automated assistance have shown where such services can be applied as an option to deliver fast assistance where the wait for an available person can be lengthy and when available can be slow to understand, and even slower to determine how to fix the offered problem (Chui et al., 2016).

Decision-making will be the last bastion of human workers, but when the Hedge Fund Managers in Stamford Connecticut. It around while the programmed trading of most traffic on the stock exchanges under code provided by the mathematicians, physicists, engineers who inhabit the work; of the "Quants", if our finances are underpinned by AI coded stock, bond, and futures trading, our day to day management decision-making seems rather mundane.

So our book intends to first present you with some of the basic elements of AI and Machine Learning, and then to show how it is currently being employed in a number of major industries in the Unites States. Figure 1.1 indicates the broad area covered by those who currently discuss AI. We discuss the general topic of deterministic systems which store the knowledge of experts and are triggered into action based upon a component of input that can be translated into an expert's action. These were initially developed in the late 1980s as expert systems with much hope for utilization, but soon faded in the 1990s. Since then, beginning in the late 1990s and early 2000s, AI emerged as a topic of much interest in companies such as Google, particularly to solve their enormous search problems, and IBM, who saw potential to employ such programs on their large computers. These projects quickly advanced toward systems that could be trained with large amounts of data whose identity was known. Neuroscience added additional knowledge of wiring of

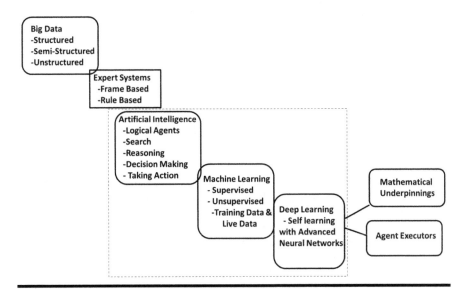

Figure 1.1 The major components that encompass Artificial Intelligence and Machine Learning.

neurons in human and animal brains (up to 100 billion neurons in humans, each with up to a thousand branches of axons that interconnect these neurons). From this insight, neural networks became the component of Machine Learning which can be taught with millions of live cases, and then begin learning on its own as it experiences live data in the situation where they are deployed. (Deep Learning then incorporated all the advancements resulting from creating increasing numbers of layers of intelligent nodes that could learn from their experiences (Aggarwal, 2018). Figure 1.1 portrays some of the components that comprise our current experiments with AI and Machine Learning.

Our book is organized with some initial chapters on the components and operation of AI and Machine Learning. These chapters follow the structure of the two books that are treated as the "bibles" in these areas: Stuart Russell and Peter Norvig's *Artificial Intelligence: A Modern Approach*, (Russell & Norvig, 2010) which is the standard textbook in virtually all universities offering AI courses, and Ian Goodfellow, Yoshua Bengio, and Aaron Courville's *Deep Learning* (Goodfellow et al., 2017), which is quickly assuming a similar stature covering Machine Learning. Other sources include Charu Aggarwal's *Neural Networks and Deep Learning* (Aggarwal, 2018), Eugene Charniak's *Introduction to Deep Learning* (Charniak, 2018), and Jeff Heaton's three-volume *Artificial Intelligence for Humans* (Heaton, 2015). Furthermore, numerous papers on these subjects are available over the Internet including Vishal Maini and Samer Sabri's very lucid *Machine Learning for Humans* (Maini & Sabri, 2017).

The initial basics chapters are followed by a series of chapters that address how and where AI is being employed by specific companies and industries. We have attempted to cover a broad spectrum of American businesses in order to demonstrate the importance and rapid deployment of resources to utilize such technologies and systems in their daily operation.

References

Aggarwal, Charu, *Neural Networks and Deep Learning*, Springer, Cham, Switzerland, 2018.

Berbazzani, Sophia, 10 Jobs Artificial Intelligence Will Replace (and 10 Jobs That Are Safe), *HubSpot*, Nov 7, 2018.

Bomey, Nathan, Special Report: Automation Puts Jobs in Peril, *USA Today*, Feb 6, 2017.

Charniak, Eugene, *Introduction to Deep Learning*, MIT Press, Cambridge, MA, 2018.

Chui, Michael, James Manyuika, and Mehdi Miremadi, *Where Machines Could Replace Humans - And Where They Can't*, McKinsey Quarterly, July 2016, https://www.mckinsey.com/business-functions/mckinsey-digital/our-insights/where-machines-could-replace-humans-and-where-they-cant-yet.

Heaton, Jeff, *Artificial Intelligence for Humans, Vol 3 Deep Learning and Neural Networks*, Heaton Research, Inc., Chesterfield, MO, 2015.

Goodfellow, Ian, Yoshua Bengio, and Aaron Courville, *Deep Learning*, MIT Press, Cambridge, MA, 2016.

Maini, Vishal and Samer Sabri, Machine Learning for Humans, August 19, 2017. https://medium.com/machine-learning-for-humans/why-machine-learning-matters-6164fafldfl2.

McKinsey, *Jobs Lost, Jobs Gained: Workforce Transitions in a Time of Automation*, McKinsey Global Institute, Dec 2017, https://www.mckinsey.com/~/media/mckinsey/featured%20insights/future%20of%20organizations/what%20the%20future%20of%20work%20will%20mean%20for%20jobs%20skills%20and%20wages/mgi-jobs-lost-jobs-gained-report-december-6-2017.ashx.

McKinsey, *Notes from the AI Frontier - Modeling the Impact of AI on the World Economy*, McKinsey Global Institute, Sep 2018.

Russell, Jon, Google's AlphGo AI Wins a Three-Match Series Against the World's Best Go Player, *TechCrunch*, May 5, 2017. https://techcrunch.com/2017/05/24/alphago-beats-planets-best-human-go-player-ke-jie/.

Russell, Stuart and Peter Norvig, *Artificial Intelligence: A Modern Approach*, 3rd ed., Pearson, Hoboken, NJ, 2010.

Chapter 2

The Basic Elements of Artificial Intelligence

Frank M. Groom
Ball State University

Contents

Introduction

As businesses recognize the breakthrough potential of Artificial Intelligence (AI) in the past decade, they have discovered that the theoretical possibilities are actually achievable with current software and hardware. From a software perspective, we have seen the IBM Deep Blue overcome world chess champion Garry Kasparov in 1997 after Kasparov won the first match in 1996. However, in 2017 Google's AI program, AlphaGo, beat Ke Jie who is arguably the best player of the most complicated game ever devised. AlphaGo was developed by DeepMind, the AI arm of Google's parent, Alphabet. Most Silicon Valley companies are placing large financial and personnel resources into not only AI research, but actually focusing on software and products that can be quickly brought to market.

Our newspapers delight in describing the successes and occasional tragedies emerging from the introduction of self-driving and assisted driving cars. The number of sensors, controllers, and communication modules offers a test-bed for a large number of AI components which the automotive industry is willing to finance. These automated components which the automotive industry is experimenting with will provide information which all technology companies will use to determine the level of control that localized and remote algorithmic software can exercise.

As these live experiments and deep research are employed, the decade of 2019–2029 is emerging as the anticipated time frame within which companies and customers could expect products that significantly rely on AI algorithms would become available and evidence some level of self-growth by means of programmed self-actuated Machine Learning which will augment the capability of AI control.

AI resides in an agent that interacts with its targeted environment by means of sensors which it either contains or is connected to, and actuators that trigger action in the environment (Heaton, 2013, 2014).

Other information used in a more delayed fashion can reside in an external solid-state disk (SSD) or disk storage which is external and mostly distant from the actual agent enacting an intelligent action.

Representation

Representing a Problem

The first step in dealing with a problem involves establishing a set of well-defined goals each with a specification of a situation and what from that situation would cause an agent to recognize it by means of its sensors, and to perform a set of actions as a consequence of such recognition. Following the establishment of goals, problem formulation involves creating a definitive link between sensor recognition and action implementation. The set of sensor stimuli, and links to a particular action set, is considered require a set of reasoning steps whose result choses one of the available senses to action links to invoke at that particular instant as the most appropriate problem formulation.

Representation of Information

All information and programs within a computer exist in the digital form (0 and 1s). Of principal importance is how much information is stored as an accessible unit, and how fast and how frequently it can be delivered to the AI agent actuator. In traditional data processing, information can be stored seconds away from the agent employing it for action. With AI enactment, the agent activator usually responds to some recognized stimulation within the time frame of nanoseconds. This requires that the employed information utilized by the actuator reside within the agent or attached to that agent. Remote data storage can host versions of that information, and prepare and download periodic updates to the remote AI agent.

Storing Knowledge

Once gathered, the "intelligence" component of AI must be stored. On the one hand, it can be stored inside the agent that actively makes use of it to address an issue or solve a problem. On the other hand, it can be stored in local but connected to the agent. Then again, it can be stored in a remote location and accessed or downloaded when needed for taking an action decision.

The intelligence can be used by a purely active agent that is either embedded in the local environment, or located close to it, or placed in a remote location. Furthermore, this agent can be a blind reactor to a stimulus or a weak or strong method-based (algorithm executing) problem solver.

Representing Knowledge

Many of the commonly employed approaches for organizing knowledge are based upon the general principles of knowledge representation used in Expert Systems. These include frame structures, scripts, objects, and conceptual graphs and semantic nets.

Frames

A classic approach for storing knowledge is using an algorithmic execution engine having a frame with a structure that contains the following components:

- A **Frame ID** to access the frame and use its enclosed information and execute its algorithm.
- The **Relationship of the Frame** to other frames – frequently implemented as a pointer.
- The **Description** of the enclosed knowledge and agent.
- The **Method** or procedure algorithm that makes use of the encoded knowledge to solve a problem or react to a stimulus and recognized situation.

Trees

Another classic storage of expert information is a tree structure. Information is identified by an ID which might logically appear as Layer 1-Key, Layer 2-Key, Layer 3-Key, and finally a Bottom Leaf-Key. A file of information organized in tree structure is accessed by the first part of the ID Key, where only matching information are selected and the others are avoided, and then it moves to the next ID Key of the branch, making decisions at each branch based upon matching the subsequent components of the ID set until it reaches the bottom level where the desired information lies. The information is obtained as an integrated set whether it be text, numeral, picture, sound, map, or other specialized characters.

Objects

An object structure is formed as a logical tree. At the top of the tree exists a Class component that contains all information shared by a number of similar Object Instances and is identified with the first characters/numbers of the overall Object ID (OID). The later part of the ID is specific to an individual instance of that object. Think of a file of professors as part of the class of professors in a school of a university. All shared information of the school's professors is stored at the school level. Shared department information might reside in a Sub-Class level extended off the school class level. Then at the bottom would exist individual clusters of information associated with Object Instances for each individual professor, containing all the details specific only to that professor (Adshead, n.d.).

Formulating Problems and Solutions

The first step in solving problems is to formulate a goal. This goal is based upon the nature of the presented problem, the situation of that problem, the elements involved, and the capability of the solving AI component. The goal, once stated, allows one to organize all the possible sequence of steps to achieve it. These steps include a specific event that triggers back to keep the process in motion. Furthermore, there may actually be many possible conclusions to a triggering event, each of which has a set of steps leading to a separate conclusion depending on the information contained in the triggering event.

Well-defined problems with known solutions are easier to program. A known trigger with a known set of parameters can be programmed to follow one of a set of sequential steps leading to a specific one of a possible set of concluding actions.

Real-world problems, on the other hand, tend to offer only partial information to the agent that is charged to deal with the problem. Generally, the agent must then carry out a decision-making process for selecting an appropriate path to pick a possible solution that has predefined probabilities based upon prior information as to the likelihood of appropriateness to each possible solution path given the inputted information and conditions. As a result, a particular chosen solution action is attained which is not deterministic, because it has not only the highest likelihood of being the correct action but also some possible likelihood of being incorrect. In dealing with such situations, it must be assured through a strong positive probability that disastrous incorrect actions are not chosen. The agent must have weights associated with each probability that protects against improper actions that have negative consequences.

Storing Knowledge and Information

Storing knowledge is necessarily connected to how we will access and find it when we need it again. We might decide to merely string one cluster or file of information after another until we exhaust the storage unit. Or we might create fixed-size fields with an ID and assemble them into a formal fixed-length record. A collection of these records can further be assembled into a Block or Table. Or if we have pictures, tunes, images, or a varying set of text or data, we might group them with an ID and lay in a string until, once again, we exhaust our storage device.

File Structures

Modern storage approaches tend to employ either a Block-level Storage approach, a File-level Storage approach, or an Object-level Storage approach. Block- and Object-level approaches are similar to and different from each other in some ways. Similarly, File- and Object-level approaches have similarities and differences between each other. However, Block- and File-level systems have major differences between them.

Block- and Object-level Storages are both based on a computer resident application program utilizing a separate File System residing on the same computer. This co-resident File System is the database manager that contains all the location and addressing information to access the required information which resides on a separate Storage Array that is reached by means of a network connecting all components of the data center. Thus in Block- and Object-level systems, the File System (database manager) on the accessing computer handles the process of determining the address and physical location of the desired blocks or objects on the storage units.

The key difference between File- and Block-level accesses is that in the File-level system, the accessing computer contains only an application program that requests the data. The actual File System (database manager) containing the details of location and address resides out on an array along with all the data. An application's data requests go out over a storage network to the Storage Array where the Resident File System programs reside. The Files system then accesses the desired file as a volume or virtual drive.

In Block-level systems, both the application program and the File System (database manager) reside together in the accessing computer. The File System contains all the information of location and address required to access the data that is stored at a distant location. Only the Block-level information required to find and access the information needs to be transferred to the remote storage controller and arrays of storage devices in order for it to locate and retrieve the requested data. The data are stored in blocks, volumes, or tables. Each block is assigned an arbitrary identifier by which it can be stored and retrieved. A common use for block storage is in the storage of databases, usually relational databases of fixed length and field records grouped in tables (Rouse, n.d.).

On the other hand, File- and Object-level Storage systems are alike in that they both organize data into files and folders in a tree-like hierarchy and provide a path to the file. They also retain a small set of descriptive data about the data that is also stored in those files (termed as "metadata"). But they differ in that the Object-level Storage system retains the File System (database manager)with the requesting applications, while the File-level system places the File System out with the data.

Although the Object- and Block-level Storage systems are similar in locating the File System with the requesting applications, they differ. While Block-level Storage arranges fixed-length and fixed-field records in Blocks for storage, an Object-level Storage system organizes data into Containers or Buckets called "Objects". These Objects reside in a flat file with a flat address space. Each added object is placed immediately after the previous one at the end of a string of such objects. All these objects then exist on the same flat, extendable, sequentially addressed space (file) (Rouse, n.d.).

Furthermore, different from a Block level's records with individually identified and accessible fields, an Object level treats each object as a complete entity. No parts can be modified, added, or subtracted from it. The object exists as a complete and unique unit. It can be stored or deleted as an entity, but can only be modified (or updated) by extracting it completely, then modifying it, and replacing it in storage with a new and updated version.

In an Object-level system, each object has a unique OID that allows a server or end user to retrieve it as an intact entity using an index to discover its exact location

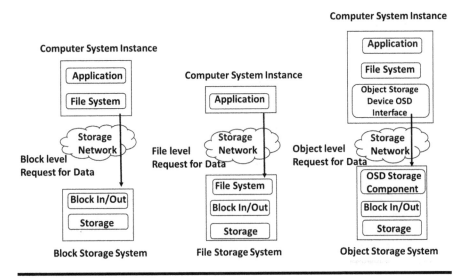

Figure 2.1   Comparison of Block-, File-, and Object-level Storages.

on the storage device. The object might contain a picture, a document, a program code, a text, or a combination of these. Thus, there is no standard size and format to these stored objects.

Users and applications access these stored objects through an application program interface (API) or by means of sending standard hypertext transfer protocol (HTTP) messages containing a seek command and subsequently retrieving the requested response back. These seek and response commands and the resultant data are transmitted over a storage network between the requesting application server and the storage device (Adshead, n.d.).

Figure 2.1 presents three types of File Access approaches: File-, Block-, and Object-level accesses.

Storage Hardware

Solid-State Disk (SSD) – Data centers currently place up to 30 processors in a rack with local solid-state storage units contained in the same rack for those computers. These racks of computers are then clustered in a row. Newer personal computers use similar solid-state storage in place of spinning disk drives. Smaller processing units are easily packaged with these chip-based storage units.

Disk arrays – Larger disk storage units contain arrays of inexpensive disks with a processor in the same unit controlling access to the enclosed disk array. In data centers, the application programs have their large databases of information stored on these disk arrays which are then accessed over a data center-wide storage network. Similar to the clustered rows of computers, disk arrays are placed in racks and then rows of these disk arrays are clustered together.

Searching for Knowledge and Actions

Searching through a database of information, possible actions, and executable code requires the use of a problem-solving agent that includes a search component. The data may be stored as a file of objects laid out sequentially, usually in a first come, first stored fashion. Such objects contain an OID and some indicators of size, metadata, and the object's knowledge and possible executable code. The location where the object has been stored is contained in an index file which is loaded in processor memory, and searched for the appropriate access location. However, usually a set of possible key words are required to identify which object is desired, and a set of synonyms for those key words must also be included so that a match can be made with the proper object stored on the file. From our experience in building Expert Systems, we have discovered that we should not expect a key word required for searching the file to be precisely provided. A proper set of commonly employed synonyms is a requirement since not everyone employs the same words for similar meanings (Russell, 2010).

An alternative structure to be searched is a tree or graph which has an entry point and then a set of expansion nodes leading to an action node at the bottom of the tree (Figure 2.2).

Breadth-First Search

With a Breadth-First Search after search entry to the initial point, the Search Process proceeds to the next Expansion State of Nodes. Instead of following any one of the Expansion items (B, C, and D), the Search Process checks with each of Nodes B, C, and D first before selecting the appropriate one to examine at the Leaf Executable level (Figures 2.3 and 2.4).

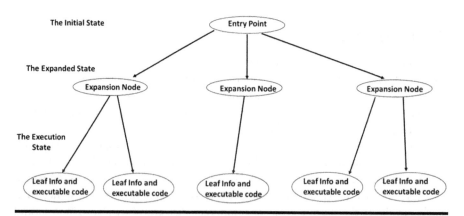

Figure 2.2   Tree structure for storing knowledge.

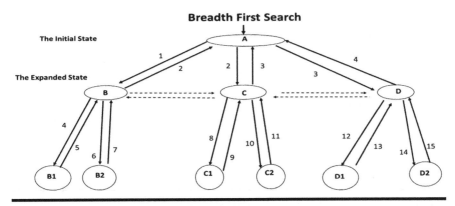

Figure 2.3   Breadth-First Search of knowledge trees.

```
            Example Breadth-First Search Code with defaults
Function Breadth-First Search [problem details] Returns [solution, failure]
Function [Recursive DFS [ ] Returns [ ]
        If [Goal Test] [node state]
                then Returns [either a Solution or a Failure to Solve]
                Else If [ ] Returns Cutoff
        Do Loop
                If Empty [] then Return Solution
                        Chose the Shallowest Node
        For Each action in Problem state
                Do Child State
                        If Child State Not explored
                                Then If Problem Goal Test [ ]
                                Then Return [Solution of Child]
                        Else
        Cutoff occurred – True or False
        For Each Action
                Do
                        If [Result = Cutoff] Then [Cutoff =true]
                        Else If then Return [Result]
                        If Cutoff occurred Then Return [Cutoff]
                                Else Return [Failure]
        Exit
```

Figure 2.4   Example of Breadth-First Search code with defaults.

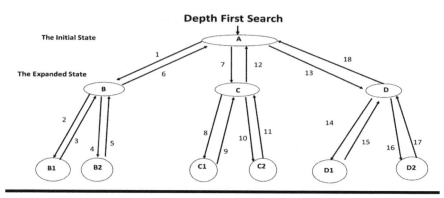

Figure 2.5   Depth-First Search of knowledge trees.

Depth-First Search

With a Depth-First Search after search entry at the initial point, the Search Process proceeds to the first Expansion State of Node. It then follows the first of the Leaf Level Expansion items (B1, and then B2). Then, the Search Process goes to the next Expansion Node C, checks each of its Leaf Nodes (C1 and C2), and finally goes to Expansion Node D and then searches each of its Leaf Nodes (D1 and D2) before returning back to the entry Node A (Figure 2.5).

Other useful extensions of these searches are Iterative Deepening Search and Lowest Cost Search algorithms. (Klein and Abbeel, n.d.)

Informed Search

Informed Searches take advantage of information available beyond that contained in the definition of the problem itself. The additional information is generally of the "cost" type where cost can be any characteristic that is desired as "best". Each node will have a "cost" value, and we search for the best cost node.

Informed Searches intend to find the first "best" node that they discover. The Best-First algorithm usually includes an additional heuristic algorithm. This employs a practical method, is not guaranteed to be either optimal, perfect, logical, or rational, but still is sufficient for achieving an immediate goal. An example of searching with a heuristic algorithm might include an "estimated" cost contained as an element in each of the leaf nodes. Then, the first one encountered that meets an estimated lowest cost appropriate for the algorithm might be considered sufficient. Early but with satisfactory stopping is expected (Seker, 2017).

Sophisticated Search

   a. Branch and Bound – This search technique combines the Depth-First simple strategy, which tends to end up with an optimal solution eventually, with a

Heuristic Search approach – most frequently using an A* technique – which tends to reduce the number of search nodes and thus the cost.

b. Direction of Search – The size of the tree one needs to search depends upon the path lengths down the tree and the branching approach one will use to leave one leg of the tree and go to another for searching. The tree or graph search can begin at a start node and search forward until reaching a goal node on the tree, or start with any goal node at the end of a tree leg and work backward to a start node. Our goal is to search from a particular starting node and search with the minimum number of branches to reach our destination. The idea of bi-directional search is to search forward and backward simultaneously until we intersect at a common node, thus determining the best path that is common from both directions.

c. Dynamic Programming is an Operations Research technique by which we heuristically decide to simplify the number of nodes available as well as use information from previous searches to simplify the search problem. By using each of a number of previous searches employed with other problems, we create a Pattern Database that allows us to minimize part of our search decisions. This should allow us to reach an approximate solution where we may choose to accept and stop or we might choose to proceed on to a better one if that is necessary. However, we must retain the location of the satisfactory solution, should none better be discovered.

Heuristic Search

As described in the Informed Search section, Heuristic Searches use available information to make a "best guess" about an efficient path to an appropriate solution node for the offered problem. Furthermore, one might employ a Heuristic Search for a simple version of a given problem, and then subsequently having solved the simple search problem, one might use that information from the simple problem's solution for the best path, cost, and goal information as a starting point for a more sophisticated algorithm to help it minimize the search path for the more difficult problem.

One of the most popular Heuristic Search algorithms is the A* Search. The A* would use information from previous searches to store a best cost for each offered path (start to goal node) at the search entry point, usually the top node of the tree structure. Then, a heuristic routine uses a simple algorithm to expand a selected path that is constrained by the requirement to minimize the cost of the search and thus picking only the least cost/least node span to research a workable solution to the problem.

Local Search Algorithms

Local Search Algorithms minimize the use of memory. They start at a single node, don't retain information of the paths searched, but chose a "best" solution among their nearest neighbors. They don't guarantee the best solution, but can quickly achieve a good solution among those close to the starting point node, if one exists.

a. Hill Climbing Simulated Annealing search follows the path at each node that offers an increasing solution value. The search terminates at a node where no further paths offer an increased value at the next following node. This is analogous to climbing a hill until a plateau is reached and terminates at the first plateau.

b. Local Beam Search starts with a set of starting nodes or "states". From each, it seeks the next improving node and stops when the best value is reached from one of the paths of the available starting nodes.

Adversarial Search and Games

A two-player game tree is structurally similar to a search tree or decision tree, with alternate moves recorded at each stage of the tree. The expected game result is Zero Sum in which if one player succeeds (wins), the other does not (loses). With a minimax algorithm, the terminal nodes at the bottom of the tree satisfy a minimax utility function which the winning player maximizes.

a. With Alpha–Beta Pruning of minimax trees, we prune away large parts of the tree that cannot possibly contribute to a successful conclusion. This technique allows minimax game approaches to be used with very large trees which couldn't possibly prove successful, so that we can reach a conclusion in a reasonable time frame.

b. With Move Ordering, it has been determined that pruning the tree effectively depends on the order in which the nodes are examined. If one looks down through the tree first and discovers some improved results, those branches can be analyzed, while those branches that tend to have successive lower nodes, which don't significantly improve the progression to success, can be eliminated from further examination.

Problem-Solving, Decision-Making, and Taking Action

Once we have searched for and found the knowledge and possible algorithm code, we might then consider what we are intending to do with that knowledge and algorithm. Do we have only partial knowledge and thus might be considering a range of possible actions? Or do we have full knowledge of the situation and the appropriate algorithm that when executed deals with the problem at hand?

Finally, many business problems do not really require the perfect solution. Frequently, they need to determine a bounding range around the possible solutions

```
function SIMPLE-PROBLEM-SOLVING-AGENT( percept) returns an action
    static: seq, an action sequence, initially empty
            state, some description of the current world state
            goal, a goal, initially null
            problem, a problem formulation
    state ← UPDATE-STATE( state, percept)
    if seq is empty then do
        goal ← FORMULATE-GOAL(state)
        problem ← FORMULATE-PROBLEM(state, goal)
        seq ← SEARCH( problem)
    action ← FIRST( seq)
    seq ← REST( seq)
    return action
```

Figure 2.6   An example of problem-solving agent. (Luger, 2009)

to a given problems. One might then either continue to attempt to narrow that bounding range around the set of potential solutions to a problem, or apply either the simplest of the solutions in the range of good solutions, the first one available, or take a further step to determine a better solution among the bounded range of good solutions appropriate for the given problem (Figure 2.6).

Reasoning

A. Reasoning with Full Knowledge – when all the information that is sufficient to trigger a given action is received, we have a straightforward link between sensing, triggering, and taking action.

B. Reasoning with Partial Knowledge – when we received only part of the information that is sufficient to take an action, we have a choice. We can either deny that action due to insufficient information available, or create a probability set. This set might be arranged following the sequence in which a series of inputs are sensed and in a particular order. We might assign a weight to each input. When we reach a given threshold, where a number of higher weights have been activated, we can conclude that the satisfaction state is achieved, because even though we have inputted only partial sensed information, predominantly the most important items have been received. On the other hand, we might receive a large number of marginally weighted pieces of information, but so many of them add up to a sum greater than our established threshold, resulting in taking the prescribed action, even though all the generally required information are not received, but most of it.

C. Probabilistic Reasoning deals with situations where the inputs are uncertain. To deal with this, we must assign probabilities associated with each input. We then construct a logic statement that collects all the received sensed inputs, programmatically calculates the most probable among them, and takes the solution action that best matches the uncertain set of inputs. Frequently, this must be sensitized by how drastic or consequential any of the actions are. We then construct negative weights associated with the most consequential actions such that a threshold must be reached combining the positive probabilities associated with the inputs minus any negative weights associated with the more consequential outcome that we are reluctant to initiate unless it is necessary. If so, we can create a range of barriers so that the input weights must overcome the effect of sizable output weights in order to trigger actions which are reluctantly taken (Heaton, 2013, 2014, 2015).

Agents Employing Reasoning and Making Decisions

From our experience in building Expert Systems (Turban, 2010) and structuring systems around Object-Oriented Programming, we have learned how to extract knowledge from "experts" in a subject, how to codify that knowledge, and what are the various ways to represent and store the acquired knowledge, and finally how to combine the stored knowledge with a set of decision-making and action taking code. We have learned how to employ Expert Systems to act as a surrogate for some of, and sometimes all of, the functions of an expert. Many of those components employed with the deterministic systems of inputs triggering specific outputs and actions associated with Expert Systems can now also be employed with the more probabilistic and highly variable problem-solving which is the realm of AI (Turban, 2010).

A. An agent is a software-driven device that perceives its environment, senses changes in that environment for which it is programmed to react to through components called sensors, and then reacts to what it has sensed by means of actuators which are used by the device to take action. The agent may be a software-programmed device that responds to the sensing, a robotic component that takes mechanical or electronic action, or a communicator that transmits packets of information as a response to what is sensed in the environment. In all such cases, the agent's function and reaction are implemented by a software program.

The set of agents that decide and execute such code can range from small units that respond to a single stimulus to larger units that have a range of inputs and a set of possible actions and whose principle function is deciding which action best matches which input stimulus. Still more complex agents must be able to make decision based upon probabilities that comprise a before state (termed as an "a priori" state), which may have some partial sets of both information and probabilities, and a subsequent afterward state (termed as an "a posteriori" state), which contains a set of subsequent information and probabilities. Such complex agents deal with the decision problem that most replicates those which a human must deal with, particularly acting in place of a human in a business decision-making situation.

In compiling a set of agents to deal with these situations, we have:

1. Logical Agents – These are the core action modules of an AI unit. They have one of a set of common architectures written in a common code (more recently Go or Python, but some with older C++ and even Java components). A library of pre-established units of code appropriate for specific actions are contained in an Action Library. This library contains a set of appropriate input codes that are coordinated with certain components of stimuli and triggers contained in an Input Library. Also contained are routines dealing with Bayesian prior (a priori) probabilities and afterward (a posteriori) conditional and distribution-specific probabilities which are stored in a probability library. Furthermore, contained are a selection of final action modules that may be employed and a set of models for other possible actions that might be taken. The Action Library is thus a complete "tool set" for constructing the logical elements for a wide range of effective agents all stored together in an Action Library. However, most actions are likely to be unique to a setting and may make use of the common action model but require unique combinations of code sequence to effectuate the specific action required for each specific set of inputs arising from the problem situation. From such available code modules and experience assembling provides a set appropriate to each problem situation, the coding part of constructing AI agents can be rather rapid. The most time-consuming work in the systems analytic elements is examining each situation where the AI agent must operate and respond to various stimuli.

2. Semantics – Many problems being addressed by AI agents do not deal with numeric information or on/off indicators, but with human-written or -spoken language. Such information must first be analyzed with parsing for identifying language structure and then finding a range of possible common words for similar terms arriving with the input. Libraries of common synonyms are constructed to enable the language of the input stimuli to be matched with the ones associated with the Logical Agent's range of possible words or expressions which are associated with and trigger a particular action.

3. Pattern, Image, Sound, and Picture Recognition Agents – A common problem facing an AI agent is receiving a string of bits, frequently in encrypted form, and once decrypted, determining the nature of the

pattern and then its actual content. The presented pattern may contain a picture, sound, or spoken or written language, or it may present a pattern of operation. Algorithms have been and are being developed to address pictures and sounds. Standard versions of presentation (jpegs, gifs, PnP, etc.) are available, with a range of size commonly associated with each expected binary pattern, and with libraries of more complicated patterns becoming available. Pattern recognition agents are tasked with addressing the most common patterns in each category, and the agents may be specialized just to handle one of these patterns. More complicated patterns are then padded of a network to specialized servers handling pattern recognition problems submitted by a distributed set of local recognition agents. These specialized agents may then take action or respond to the local agent to take the appropriate action locally.

4. Propositional Theorems – The small, single action agent, the more complex agent dealing with probabilistic situations and possible actions, the language-oriented agents, and the Pattern Recognition Agents present unique difficulties for the constructor of an AI agent but each has some unique structural elements that allow for some special model versions appropriate to each. The difficulty arises when the required agent must deal with a combination of inputs and reasoning associated with a number or all of these object model issues. However, we can at least start by having useful models and algorithmic code appropriate for each and then rely on the experience, insight, and creativity of the coder to successfully achieve the objective.

B. Reasoning with Partial Knowledge – When only a portion of the information we need is available, we still have some options for reaching a conclusion. One approach comes from the discipline of Operations Research. The approach is to use the available information and structure a boundary around the problem which separates all the areas which our known information eliminates as a possible solution to our problem. This leaves us with solution areas comprised of boundary possibles, but less likely ones and a set of inner ones which are the most likely. We then need to make a determination as to how precise our solution needs to be. In many cases, getting the absolute correct answer is not noticeably different in outcome from getting any other ones of the possibles. If the perfect answer is 100 and answers between the range of 80 and 120 provide reasonably the same outcome, then the precision of our solution reasoning is not really required. Any solution that is not eliminated by the known information set may be satisfactory for addressing our problem. This may be especially true in a situation which is addressed in steps with a possible correction available as each succeeding step is taken.

C. Probabilistic Reasoning – We may have some ability to derive probability distributions associated with our available information such that we can weight each aspect with a likelihood number that allows us to collectively weight the collection of information by the associated item weights and reach a more probabilistic outcome than the more simplified Partial Knowledge approach. We can weight each component of known knowledge and provide a probabilistic weight for those items where we have partial but uncertain elements. Combining the weighted components gives us a more realistic view of the correct answer and allows us to go through a process of cycling through a series of possible modifications and seeing how they change our outcome. This process involves the human evaluator. However, Machine Learning with Training Data Sets goes through a similar process of gradually approaching a workable or even best solution based upon a gradual testing of the results of various learning and changed outcome (Heaton, 2013, 2014, 2015).

D. Steps in the Algorithm Process
   1. Initialization Step – In this first step, the reasoning system must make a judgment as to the type of analytic process most appropriate to the presented problem. Many of these will utilize clustering as an initial step and thus require that we choose among a possible range of Clustering Algorithms. One common technique is K-Means Clustering.
   2. Assignment Step – In this step, we proceed through a process of assigning the data associated with our presented problem into one or more of a set of possible clusters. For example, K-Means Clustering uses random assignment to the clusters or assigning them to the cluster closest to their average value (the Forgy method which looks for where there is a dense cluster of numbers and picks, the densest is the average).
   3. The Update Step – The steps of the reasoning process are repeated, updating the average values and gradually narrowing the range of the distributions around those averages until a satisfactory conclusion is reached.

E. Some Specialized Problems – There are a number of common problems associated with many businesses which Operations Research and Expert Systems people have faced and addressed for many years. Most famous of these is the "Traveling Salesman Problem", which not only presents a best route-finding problem, but can also be extended to many best conclusion problems. Furthermore, for many business situations, finding the exact, perfect solution is really not absolutely necessary. We might be quite satisfied to merely bound the problem space in such a way that a small number of solutions may be determined, anyone of which might offer a satisfactory answer. The approach taken is to break the offered problem into a set of smaller problems. In solving the small problems, much of the results can be reused for other small problems, reducing considerably the amount of processing required. The field of Dynamic Programming from Operations Research finds an acceptable solution rather than attempting to find the exact, perfect solution to the offered problem.

F. Training Sets – Training is the process of exposing the algorithmic system to a sequential set of situations with their associated data such that a gradually more accurate algorithm is achieved which more accurately satisfies the solution requirement for a set of known problem situations.

Sets of data used to train an AI system are generally separated by the type of Machine Learning that is incorporated into the AI system. Unsupervised learning systems frequently attempt to classify subjects or situations into separate categories or groups. We generally do not need to do any special pre-processing, such as normalizing the data from its usual range from low to high, to a range above and below a mean of zero, or providing tags for the individual sets. We merely take a vector of data and compare it to a set of standard data, and then assign it to one of those data types or to a new type of its own while updating our training standard sets.

Supervised training data contain a set of known input data and a set of known output data. The training process then consists of running the data against the pattern recognition agent's decision algorithm and determining how often and for what reason the correct output was chosen for the particular submitted input.

Resolution, Reaching Reasoned Conclusions, and Taking Appropriate Action

Resolution occurs after the agent proceeds through a set of clauses, satisfies the conditions of each clause, and reaches a stage of reasoned closure. From this stage, a set of available actions are presented, and based upon the final reasoning step, the agent determines which of the available actions have all of the pre-conditioned reasoning steps satisfied, such that the action is the correct response to the presented set of conditions. Where probabilities have been appropriate for reaching a particular conclusion, an additional cautionary step must be invoked to avoid conclusions resulting in inappropriate and possibly disastrous results which might be chosen due to probabilistic reasoning. Once all the pre-conditions are satisfied, the agent either directly takes action or sends a message to another agent that awaits the triggering event of that transmitted signal.

References

Adshead, Antony, Storage 101: Object Storage versus Block and File, *Computer Weekly*, n.d., www.computerweekly.com/feature/Storage-101-Object-storage-vs-block-vs-file.

Heaton, Jeff, *Artificial Intelligence for Humans Vol 1: Fundamental Algorithms*, Heaton Research, Chesterfield, MO, 2013.

Heaton, Jeff, *Artificial Intelligence for Humans Vol 2: Nature-Inspired Algorithms*, Heaton Research, Chesterfield, MO, 2014.

Heaton, Jeff, *Artificial Intelligence for Humans Vol 3: Deep Learning and Neural Networks*, Heaton Research, Chesterfield, MO, 2015.

Klein, Dan and Pieter Abbeel, *Artificial Intelligence CS188*, University of California, Berkeley, n.d., http://ai.berkeley.edu.

Luger, George, *Artificial Intelligence, Structures and Strategies for Complex Problem Solving*, Pearson Education, Addison Wesley Publishing, 2009.

Rouse, Margaret, Block Storage, TechTarget, n.d., https://searchstorage.techtarget.com/definition/block-storage.

Russell, Stuart and Peter Norvig, *Artificial Intelligence: A Modern Approach*, 3rd ed., Pearson, Irving, TX, 2010.

Seker, Sadi Evern, *Introduction to Artificial Intelligence SC290*, Smith College, Department of Computer Science, Spring 2017, http://sadievrenseker.com.

Turban, Efraim, *Decision Support and Expert Systems*, 9th ed., MacMillan, Prentice Hall, NJ, 2010.

Chapter 3

Artificial Intelligence and the Cloud

Ryan Suter
enVista

Contents

As technology continues to grow and our computing capabilities expand, so too does the definition of artificial intelligence (AI) as you may have noticed already. One of the newest forms of AI is the combination of AI with cloud technologies. The combination of AI and the cloud allows for users to use all the tools and services of the cloud platform with the support of AI from high-level facial recognition to low-level data manipulation. AI within the cloud is considered by many as the next step in computing technology. As our understanding of both AI and cloud computing grows, we will see the portfolios of AI vendors grow as well.

Some believe that AI made its way into the cloud in 2017. However, some of the first recorded cases of AI in the cloud start back in the early 2000s and became popularized by IBM's Watson. Watson was originally a computing system capable of answering complex questions using data sets housed in the cloud and other data storage locations. Its first major use was in the show *Jeopardy!* as one of the contestants. Watson hears keywords and phrases and then uses IBM's DeepQA software plus Apache UIMA (unstructured information management architecture) to find information stored in the cloud to formulate an answer. Today, Watson also provides many other services. It has the capability to do extremely complex tasks, from writing code to everyday tasks like predicting the weather and tax preparation.

The combination of AI and services in the cloud allows Watson to do all of these tasks and get better at these tasks the more it does them. Because there is an almost unlimited amount of storage space in the cloud, the AI running within Watson and other AI continues to learn better ways to do tasks and stores that information back to the cloud for later use (Bagachi et al., 2012).

AI in the cloud can do more than just generate answers on a game show. Many different companies are already coming up with their own AI combined with cloud services. The combination of these two services is known as AI as a service or AIaaS. Companies such as Amazon, Google, and Microsoft have already begun to start their own line of AIaaS. Among some of the top AIaaS currently are IBM's Watson, Amazon Machine Learning, Microsoft Cognitive Services, and Google Cloud Machine. Salesforce has also created their version of AIaaS combining cloud platform as a service and software as a service with AI to create myEinstein. Larger companies are currently the front-runner with this new service as it is very costly. Many AI providers are also being purchased by these companies as well to create better integrated systems. This helps organizations by providing more services; however, the cost of these services will continue to grow as the market is controlled by only a handful of providers. Fortunately, AIaaS allows for the services to be well researched and tested before becoming part of a company. The cloud portion allows for remote testing to be done, while the AI algorithms allow for the services to be run virtually anywhere. With the rise in AI and the current successful state of cloud computing, it is likely that more AIaaS providers will come to fruition in the next few years (Harvey, 2018).

Cloud computing has already changed the way businesses store and use data in drastic ways. However, cloud computing is still a relatively new technology. Companies need to continue to look for ways to advance this technology so that it will reach its full potential. Adding AI is a step toward that full potential. The cloud provides the AI with information and what it needs to learn, and in turn, AI can provide more data back to the cloud. These technologies benefit each other and make the technology easier to use. For example, AI uses up a lot of computing power, making it almost impossible to run on many at home devices. However, if the AI is housed inside the cloud, that gives the user more computing power while being able to utilize the services without any expensive hardware upgrades. When a company has success with these new AI technologies, having them work with the cloud will also allow for the expansion and scalability of these researched services. AI and the cloud also provide companies with a way to access new AIaaS technologies, without any large investment of having these technologies housed in servers on-site because the hardware and software are provided by the cloud vendor. This allows companies to fully experiment with AIaaS products without the worry that next year will bring something more innovative than the currently housed AIaaS product (Snow, 2017).

People skilled at using AI in the cloud are not abundant. Finding people that can utilize these services together, while still not having an enormous wage to pay out, is unlikely. Since these AI technologies are housed in the cloud, they provide a unique opportunity for companies to train their own employees rather than search for the rare skills needed to run these products. Cloud vendors are offering their clients AI services that teach people how to best utilize the services they need. These AI technologies, over time, will learn to generate images, learning modules, and even speech into their own applications so that when they are in use, the AI walks the user through the process. Over time, there will also be services created that teach users how to utilize AIaaS, similar to the way cloud vendors train users to work with cloud services now (Google, n.d.a,b).

AI also has benefits to the vendors as well. Vendors use the AI to help with tasks that teams of people would normally be assigned to. Amazon uses its AI service "Macie" to automatically help secure data stored in its instances (Lardniois, 2017). Oracle utilizes its AI in its database software to automatically manage and improve itself while creating an autonomous database. Salesforce has also started to embed "Einstein" into all its software to automate daily processes. Many other companies have already started to follow suit as well, embedding AI, like Einstein, straight into their software to help automate daily tasks and provide higher-level customer experiences (Salesforce Einstein, n.d.).

The benefits of AI combined with the cloud are vast and still growing. There are many different services vendors are offering to the public, and each one is unique. Currently, there are only a handful of companies offering AIaaS for the public and a lot more that are in the testing phase. It is important to remember that there are differences in what AIaaS is being provided and this can be broken down into two different categories: services that help benefit the cloud and services housed in the cloud that benefit the consumer. There are many more services offered through these cloud vendors than there are services for cloud vendors. Depending on the vendor and the service chosen, companies can utilize these services in multiple areas of their organization. It is just a matter of what is needed and how you want to work the AIaaS into an organization's business plan (Harvey, 2018).

Of all the AI services provided by vendors, the most popular service, and often how AI works, is machine learning. The four largest AIaaS providers (Amazon, Google, Microsoft, IBM) all have some form of machine learning service they provide to customers. Machine learning is inherently what it sounds like; your machines have the ability to learn. Machine learning can be utilized in many ways by data scientists and engineers. What it does is use complex algorithms or instructions programmed into the technology to automatically build analytical models. These algorithms allow the AI to learn about the data that is present and can identify unknown patterns and make its own predictions about the data without the need for a user to program the machine to look for these patterns.

Machine learning allows for many different levels of learning. What this means is that the AI in place can be told to learn and be fully supervised by the programmer all the way to completely unsupervised. Fully supervised would make the AI only look for data patterns which is told by the programmer. Unsupervised would allow the AI to find and make decisions itself based on the information in a given database. Machine learning is a great tool for data analysts because it recognizes what it is programmed to look for and can uncover hidden relationships within the data presented (SAS, n.d.).

It can be extremely difficult to understand and program AI to enable machine learning. This makes it difficult for companies to be able to locate AI-savvy employees and to afford these employees as well. There is also the difficulty of being able to "train" your AI. However, services like Amazon SageMaker allow for data models to be created easily, to train your AI to detect the data patterns you want it to find. Some services also provide user training and show tips to teach the user about the next steps they should take to implement the AI service (Miller, 2017).

In order to understand how AI in the cloud works with other AIaaS, it is important to understand what AI deep learning is and what it does for the AI technology. Deep learning is a form of machine learning that does not rely on task-oriented programmed algorithms, but uses data stored inside of the technology, like the cloud, to create learned data representation algorithms. Think of this as how your own brain works. As you grow up, you learn more and that information is stored inside of your brain. When you need information, your brain gets a signal and the information stored in your brain formulates a response. For AI, the brain is the cloud database and all the information needed for responses are stored inside of it. This is also the idea behind neural networks or a computer system designed after the human brain. Deep learning can be used in many different settings from customer relationship management to toxicology and medical predictions (Tenuto, 2015).

One of the most popular AI technologies that utilizes deep learning is speech recognition. Again, the largest AIaaS vendors have some form of this service available to their customers. Google and Amazon have taken this technology and made it a simple way for users to have the benefits of AI in the home. Speech recognition is the technology behind Amazon's "Alexa" and Google's "Google Home". The AI behind them are known as Amazon Lex and Google Speech API (application program interface). The success of both of these technologies has helped the AI industry to really boom in recent years and made AI available as an at-home product.

Amazon Lex has become popular for its ability to transform a house into a "smart home" for a relatively cheap price. This AI technology actually utilizes two different kinds of AI to function: automatic speech recognition (ASR) and natural language understanding (NLU). The ASR allows for the conversion of speech to text, while the NLU allows for intent to be given to the text. Lex allows businesses to create user-friendly applications with extremely effective chatbots. The combination of this AI technology with the cloud allows for quick scalability and a database large enough to house all of the information needed to run this technology. This same technology is used across Google, Microsoft, and IBM technology to allow for the creation of cognitive functions onto business applications. Along with these services, there are services to aid in the creation and implementation of these services within applications such as Apache MXNet, Azure Bot Services, and many different IBM Watson APIs (Amazon, n.d.).

Another AIaaS technology that is becoming more popular is cloud security through AI. Amazon has again been a front-runner in this area with its release of Amazon Macie. However, Oracle has also been created and implemented cloud security solutions through its cloud access security broker (CASB) services. These services are run using machine learning in relatively the same way. AIaaS cloud security works by monitoring the data that is told as important by you. The AI is programmed to understand where all of your most important information is stored. It then creates relationships between who normally accesses the information and what path is taken to access the information. It also assesses the location of the user trying to access the information and the times of access. If any of these situations are out of the ordinary for the user, an alert is set and the service takes appropriate action to shut down the database the attacker would be trying to access. The AI is constantly running, making it easier to monitor network activity at any time of the day. These services not only monitor outside attacks, but they can be programmed to monitor an employee's activities as well. For instance, if a user tries to put data that was listed as private into an instance or database that is public, Macie will notify the user of the problem and why it is blocking that action. The AI security can also be used for compliance. If data is needed to be stored in certain locations for compliance reasons, it will notify the user that they are not storing the information properly and help resolve the issue. Finally, this AIaaS can be programmed to act against security threats when detected. These can be small warnings like a forced password reset, all the way to resetting access controls based on the threat detected. With cloud security being a major deterrent for businesses looking to migrate to the cloud, services like these can be a helpful tool to alleviate those concerns (Walker, 2017).

AI in the cloud is still a very new service. This creates an emerging market where large cloud vendors and smaller technology companies can both succeed in creating revolutionary new services. It also allows companies that normally do not work with the cloud to research into new areas within the cloud. These new technologies will continue to advance the popularity of AI within the business and at-home market.

Adobe has taken advantage of this emerging market by combing AI with its Creative Cloud platform. Adobe Sensei was released as an AI service with their Creative Cloud to assist users in automating the tasks they would normally do on a daily basis. It currently runs on all Creative Cloud applications; however, Adobe is looking to expand to other services like Adobe I/O. Adobe I/O will help application developers in creation of a company's application by being embedded into application programming interfaces. The AI will assist in image correction, facial recognition, and any other creative tasks that users would have had to do manually. Adobe Sensei has been released for about a year, but Adobe has stated that they plan to continue with service creation using the Adobe Sensei technology (Adobe, n.d.).

Huawei is also utilizing AI in their cloud BU technology to help boost their enterprise intelligence products. These solutions focus heavily on larger manufacturing and product creation organizations that Huawei felt was being neglected by the cloud vendors. This AIaaS technology offers basic platforming and application programming interface services like deep learning and visual recognition. What separates Huawei from other AIaaS vendors is their ability to create scenario-specific solutions for these types of organizations. By putting their AIaaS solution inside of all their processes, customers now have AI end to end during the supply-chain process. Huawei is even creating intelligent packaging for their customers to keep everything running with these services. These services allow the AI to find abnormalities in the data flow and supply-chain, and make corrections for optimal business flow. This technology is also utilized for goods that need to meet compliance standards and can be kept under watch by the AIaaS as well. Huawei plans to implement this technology in their Cloud BU platform going forward in hopes that it will improve and inspire other companies to look into intelligent services (Huawei, 2017).

Large AIaaS providers have also created new services and products. Google is currently beta testing a service they call Cloud TPU (tensor processing unit). A TPU is an AI and machine learning accelerator. It functions in the same way as an application-specific integrated circuit (ASIC). ASIC functions similarly to microchips; however, instead of processing many general-purpose functions, they only process one specific function. This makes the process run much faster than if the processor had to run multiple tasks at one time. This same technology is one technique people use to mine Bitcoin. Instead of using it to mine cryptocurrencies, Google uses them in their AIaaS platform to accelerate machine learning and data training (Techopedia, n.d.). This could make the training of data go from taking a few days to a week. Initially, the technology was available only for some users on the market, but was made available to everyone in the last half of 2018 according to Google. Cloud TPU has the possibility of making one of the most difficult tasks for AI and making it a shorter process, allowing for the companies to have more time to train and run AI services (Osborne, 2016).

Another emerging AI service is the ability for machines to perceive emotion. IBM has started a service through their Watson line of AIaaS known as Watson Empathy or Watson Tone Analyzer. This service uses linguistic analysis to detect emotion and language tones in spoken to written format (IBM, n.d.). This service is twofold: on one side, your customer's emotions are better analyzed by your machines. This allows for better responses and more positive customer interaction. On the other side, it allows a company to better format the communication they have with their customers. It will analyze how words are written and how they can be received by the customer, making sure that you do not write something the customer may see as offensive or misinterpret the message. This service allows organizations to embed this AIaaS into their products and offers API developer tools. Watson Empathy could greatly improve an organization's call center or automated customer responses. It can also analyze social platforms and determine what people are saying and how they feel about your organization online. Overall, this product will continue to advance the customer service industry and provide enhanced customer interactions (IBM Cloud Docs, 2018).

With all the benefits of AI in the cloud, there are still some problems with this area. Like many other areas of robotics, job security is a concern for people in this field. With AI doing everything from complex to menial tasks, people working in these areas could be affected by the introduction of this technology. Not only could this cause loss of jobs, it could make finding a job much harder as well. With positions being replaced by AI, the reduction of available jobs is imminent. While many industries will be affected by the introduction of AI services, a new industry will be formed. AI does not automatically run itself. It can still make errors and needs to be monitored closely. It also needs to be researched as it is still in its infancy. Just like with the automobile industry, skilled workers may lose their jobs, but a whole robotics field was created in the process (Patrizio, 2016).

Just like any other technology, AI in the cloud still has some security risks. In fact, when AIaaS was becoming popular, security was not a foreseen risk because the field was so new. However, cyberterrorists and hackers are becoming more interested and skilled in the area and can cause large problems in AI-driven systems. Almost all AI attacks are done by "fooling" a system. Since the systems are designed to obey the commands they are given, when an attack occurs, the AI accepts what it is told. This could cause issues like the misinterpretation of traffic laws by AI-powered vehicles and misdiagnosis by an AI-powered medical facility to even something small like bypassing a spam filter. While AIaaS continues to grow, so will the field of AI security. As the industry sees more and more attacks happening, mitigation and threat response features will need to become standard (Polyakov, 2018).

Another foreseen problem in the area of AI and the cloud is information bias. Information bias is caused by the data that is being used to train our AI systems being out of date or untrustworthy. For example, imagine AI being used to solve a crime where the input is taken from information that is collected from 1950 to 1990. For the field of criminology, this time period of crime was heavily influenced by the large amount of drugs in the United States. Not only that, but the information is nearly 30 years old. This could extend into AI determining the likelihood of a crime offender reoffending. With data that is too old or biased based on the time period, we could see AI creating scenarios that are unfair to our justice system. Currently, AI is not able to pick up on unforeseen biases and the people inputting the information are not picking up on these biases either. As AI begins to expand, it is likely that these biases will cause greater problems and a solution may come in the form of regulations (Knight, 2017).

Finally, AI is not perfect and can make mistakes. Not every scenario can be planned for and how AI makes its decisions is much different from how humans do. There would be hundreds of situations that AI was not programmed to respond to and it will cause serious trust issues with the technology. For example, if an AI-powered car holding four passengers is about to hit a car carrying ten people or hit a brick wall, how it makes that decision may not be programmed. Even as humans, we have trouble making a decision in that situation. These problems go much deeper than that. The company Uber had a problem with its AI algorithm recently during a terrorist situation. The AI dramatically increased its prices based on the large volume of calls coming from the area the terrorists were attacking because hundreds of people were trying to flee using their service. The AI did what it was programmed to do, basing prices off of availability and necessity. As humans, we understand that in these situations you cannot increase those prices out of morality. The trust in AI here was broken, and it forced Uber to reevaluate its systems (Verdict, 2017).

It is important to remember that AI is still in its infancy. With the cloud helping AI to become a more viable technology, the increase in its uses and the research done in this field will increase exponentially. Companies, large and small, are already developing and creating new ways to implement this technology that extends past using AI for smart cars or robots. AIaaS can help drive business from data analytics to customer service. The emerging field will help create jobs and automate processes for a better business world. While AIaaS still has its problems like data bias and cost, research is being done to help alleviate these issues. The cloud is allowing for that alleviation to happen. With the ability to create and research in a low-cost environment, this technology will thrive. As the technology grows, so too will the solutions to AIaaS. It is important to embrace this technology now to stay ahead in the fast-paced field that is technology.

References

Adobe. (n.d.) *Adobe Sensei brings Intelligence to Experiences.* Retrieved from www.adobe.io/apis/cloudplatform/sensei.html.

Amazon. (n.d.) *Amazon Lex.* Retrieved from https://aws.amazon.com/lex/?nc2=h_a1.

Anyoha, R. (2017, August 28) *The History of Artificial Intelligence.* Retrieved from http://sitn.hms.harvard.edu/flash/2017/history-artificial-intelligence/.

Bagachi, S., Ferrucci, D., Gondek, D., Levas, A., Mueller, E. (2012, August 7). *Watson: Beyond Jeopardy!* Retrieved from www.sciencedirect.com/science/article/pii/S0004370212000872.

Google. (n.d.a) *Learning with Google AI.* Retrieved from https://ai.google/education/#?modal_active=none.

Google. (n.d.b) *Speech-To-Text.* Retrieved from https://cloud.google.com/speech-to-text/.

Harvey, C. (2018, January 25) *AI in the Cloud Boosts Cloud Performance.* Retrieved from www.datamation.com/cloud-computing/ai-in-the-cloud-boosts-cloud-performance.html.

Huawei. (2017, September 15) *Huawei Debuts its Innovative Enterprise Intelligence Solution and Positions Huawei Cloud as an Enabler of Intelligent World.* Retrieved from www.huawei.com/en/press-events/news/2017/9/Huawei-Enterprise-Intelligence-Solution.

IBM. (n.d.) *Tone Analyzer*. Retrieved from www.ibm.com/watson/services/tone-analyzer/.

IBM Cloud Docs (2018, April 6) *Tone Analyzer: About*. Retrieved from https://console.bluemix.net/docs/services/tone-analyzer/index.html#about.

Knight, W. (2017, October 3) *Forget Killer Robots-Bias is the Real AI Danger*. Retrieved from www.technologyreview.com/s/608986/forget-killer-robotsbias-is-the-real-ai-danger/.

Lardniois, F. (2017, August 14) *Amazon Macie helps businesses protect their sensitive data in the cloud*. Retrieved from https://techcrunch.com/2017/08/14/amazon-macie-helps-businesses-protect-their-sensitive-data-in-the-cloud/.

Miller, R. (2017, November 29) *AWS releases SageMaker to make it easier to build and deploy machine learning models*. Retrieved from https://techcrunch.com/2017/11/29/aws-releases-sagemaker-to-make-it-easier-to-build-and-deploy-machine-learning-models/.

Osborne, J. (2016, August 22) *Google's Tensor Processing Unit explained: this is what the future of computing looks like*. Retrieved from www.techradar.com/news/computing-components/processors/google-s-tensor-processing-unit-explained-this-is-what-the-future-of-computing-looks-like-1326915.

Patrizio, A. (2016, July 7) *Pros and Cons of Artificial Intelligence*. Retrieved from www.datamation.com/applications/pros-and-cons-of-artificial-intelligence.html.

Polyakov, A. (2018, February 20) *How AI-Driven Systems Can Be Hacked*. Retrieved from www.forbes.com/sites/forbestechcouncil/2018/02/20/how-ai-driven-systems-can-be-hacked/#1235900679df.

Salesforce Einstein. (n.d.) *With Salesforce Einstein, the World's #1 CRM is Now the World's Smartest CRM*. Retrieved from www.salesforce.com/products/einstein/overview/.

SAS. (n.d.) *Machine Learning: What It is and Why it Matters*. Retrieved from www.sas.com/en_us/insights/analytics/machine-learning.html.

Snow, J. (2017, December 29) *2017: The Year AI Floated into the Cloud*. Retrieved from www.technologyreview.com/s/609646/2017-the-year-ai-floated-into-the-cloud/.

Techopedia. (n.d.) *Application-Specific Integrated Circuit (ASIC)*. Retrieved from www.techopedia.com/definition/2357/application-specific-integrated-circuit-asic.

Tenuto, J. (2015, August 13) *Why You Should Use Open Data to Hone Your Machine Learning Models*. Retrieved from www.figure-eight.com/why-you-should-use-open-data-to-hone-your-machine-learning-models/.

Verdict. (2017, June 12) *Uber's Algorithms: Artificial Intelligence Problems are Laid Bare during a Crisis*. Retrieved from www.verdict.co.uk/stupidity-artificial-intelligence-wake-terror-attack/.

Walker, T. (2017, August 14) *Launch-Hello Amazon Macie: Automatically Discover, Classify, and Secure Content at Scale*. Retrieved from https://aws.amazon.com/blogs/aws/launch-amazon-macie-securing-your-s3-buckets/.

Chapter 4

Artificial Intelligence Security Threats

Ryan Suter
enVista

Contents

Artificial intelligence (AI) has been a hot topic in technology for decades. AI is described as any technology that can mimic human thought or action (Anyoha, 2017). This definition has changed many times since its creation, and the way we see AI now is not the way many other generations have described it. The idea of AI started in the 1600s when ancient mathematicians wanted to create a machine that would solve complex mathematical equations for them. Today, we know these machines as calculators. Some even believe that AI started long before that with the idea of clocks or a device that could tell time for humans outside of the sun's location. Modern AI started in the 1950s with scientists that wanted to create an artificial brain. As a result of their research, we received the world's first artificial programming in the form of a game of checkers where your computer opponent adapts to your play style and learns to play better the more games it goes through.

Currently, we see AI in many different devices and machines. There are AI-powered cars and thermostats and even packaging. As the trend for AI continues to grow, technologists find it harder to be able to secure all of these devices. Cybersecurity has been a fast-growing field for many generations and will continue to grow just as fast as the industry itself. As AI starts to blossom, what can happen when hackers and cyberterrorists get into these AI-powered technologies?

These people and groups are finding more ways to exploit AI that is far beyond just stealing data. There is even the potential to crash an AI-powered vehicle or tamper with an AI-powered medical device. There is also the idea that AI can actually make attacks even better. By utilizing AI, hackers are able to create smarter schemes and more advanced attacks. Unfortunately, malicious attacks are being developed faster than the defense systems can be made. It will be the responsibility of the industry to be prepared for these attacks and get ahead of the threats being created.

There are three distinct categories when discussing AI and security: hacking AI, AI attacks, and AI security. First, AI can be hacked on its own. AI is essentially like all other programs on a device. It has code and other technologies already in place. AI gets hacked in the same way how the other devices are already being hacked. That being said, AI does have the ability to auto-generate security measure if a suspected hack is happening. This makes it a little more difficult to take control of. Taking control of AI is just one of the ways hackers are exploiting it. Unfortunately, there are many more severe ways AI can actually be manipulated (Knight, 2016).

AI does not actually think. What AI does is look for patterns in programmed data. Since this is the way AI is designed, one of the most common ways hackers are exploiting it is by skewing or tampering with data. This can be done in many ways to many different types of AI services. For AI that is looking for patterns, one threat could be the injection of incorrect data. This could destroy years' worth of collecting data in a matter of minutes. It also forces data analysts to have to go back through their data to ensure what they are producing has not been tampered with. This type of attack would be especially problematic in predictive analytics. For example, a person or a company wants to use AI to predict stock pricing. The system they are using has been tampered with and stocks with bad predictions now look like you should be putting money into them. To the AI, it is doing exactly what it is being told. However, the original intent of the system has completely been reworked to go with whatever the hacker decides. It also has the potential to turn into a new form of ransomware. The AI can be told to encrypt data, making it unavailable to the company or user. We will see attacks like these result in huge losses in profits due to the misuse of data in the near future (Drinkwater, 2018).

The second major topic when discussing AI and security is utilizing AI to hack or attack. This has been an increasingly popular threat that businesses and technologists are trying to prepare for. Some researchers even believe that the first waves of AI-powered attacks will start happening within the next 12 months. One way attackers can use AI for hacking is by utilizing AI to help create undetectable malware. Malware in itself is not a new threat. It takes attackers a long time to produce the scripts necessary and needs many other tools for the malware to be effective.

AI not only helps make the scripts at an accelerated rate, but it can also make them stronger and undetectable to detection systems. This type of malware was first used in 2017 when a group of researchers created malware that was not only undetectable to software, but also undetectable to machine-learning detection systems.

Endgame, an IT security company, also created undetectable malware using the OpenAI framework. This malware changes its binaries to seem like they are coming from a legitimate source. These attacks are increasingly threatening, and some researchers are predicting the rise of machine-learned polymorphic malware, or malware that can frequently change its identifiable features, in the near future (Lord, 2017).

Botnets are another malicious attack that have been around for quite some time. As we begin the Internet of Things (IoT) device era, these attacks can be on a much larger scale. Researchers are not only predicting larger attacks by zombie machines, but the zombies will be smarter due to the embedded AI within them. These cluster of smart IoT devices will form a hivenet. The hivenet will be able to communicate and share information with each other automatically. They will also be able to take action without the need for a command by the attack herder. These devices will grow quickly as swarms and be able to attack many victims in a short amount of time. Researchers warn that this swarm-style technology sounds like something out of a movie, but ensure that it is a very real threat (Fortinet, 2017).

Spear phishing is one of the most common cyberattacks used today. The attacker takes over a host that may seem like a legitimate source, like a coworker. Then, the attacker sends out an email or link that seems like a legitimate link coming from a trusted person. Once the link is downloaded, the machine becomes infected. As simple as it sounds, it is extremely effective because it preys on the trust of the user. AI can strengthen this attack by utilizing algorithms to create better schemes based on failed attempts. There are already algorithms designed to make AI-powered chatbots, and responses sound more like they are coming from a real person (IBM Watson Empathy). That same algorithm can produce an email that seems even more like it is coming from a person and if the attack does not work, the algorithm improves on its own speech or text. This also allows for attackers to send phishing messages without controlling a user because the emails will seem like they are coming from a legitimate source due to the language used by the AI. Researchers have conducted this type of attack and found that its success rate is between 30% and 60%. With that type of success rate, this attack can become even more troublesome for businesses and individual users than it already is (Seymour and Tully, n.d.).

CAPTCHA is a system that stops non-human entrance into specific sites. Users have probably been asked to verify that they are "not a robot". AI has been used to break this system as early as 2012. Google even developed a more advanced version of CAPTCHA after researchers broke the first system with an almost 90% success rate. Since the redevelopment of CAPTCHA, AI has advanced enough to even break the most modern forms of CAPTCHA, and in 2016, researchers developed an AI algorithm that could break the new system with an almost 100% success rate (Keromytis, Polakis, Sivakorn, 2016).

There have been some attacks already using AI. Fortunately, most of the attacks happening right now are controlled or being done to help companies prepare for these new AI-powered attacks. The Google Brain team has developed a way to "doop" AI image recognition. This technology may not seem like the biggest problem since it is mostly used for facial recognition. However, image recognition is a main AI technology in almost all smart vehicles. The Google Brain team showed that by placing an image on top of another image, you could trick the AI into thinking an image is something else. These images are not always able to be seen by the human eye, but can be picked up by AI technology. Google Brain had the idea that they could hack an electronic billboard and insert an invisible image to tell AI-powered cars to increase their speed or even stop. If something like that happened on the highway, it could spell disaster for the people around the vehicle. Google Brain also created a foil that could do the same thing for billboards that could not be hacked. With so many smart vehicles in development, this is a huge concern for drivers and should be an even bigger concern for car companies (Smith, 2018).

This same threat can have a big impact on the medical industry as well. AI is becoming much more popular in the prediction of disease and the analysis of medical images. Researchers have found that by tricking the AI's algorithm, you can make the AI predict a disease that the patient may not even have symptoms of. Fortunately, a well-educated doctor should not base his/her decisions off of the predictions of a machine. However, AI has been utilized and continues to help recognize diseases like cancer in medical images. Earlier in this chapter, we discussed how Google Brain developed a system to "doop" AI image recognition. This same idea can also trick the AI when looking for diseases. The effects of this type of attack can be deadly to the patient, especially when some diseases can go undetected by even the best doctors with the best imaging technology. The effects of this type of attack could not hurt the reputation of doctors and hospitals, and it could even cause the death of very ill patients. As AI becomes more integrated into the medical field, a point needs to be made that AI, while a great tool, cannot be fully relied upon (Polyakov, 2018).

AI has also been used to create fake images and videos as well as to generate voices that sound like real people. Researchers believe this will be utilized by countries to spread misinformation to people, especially around voting season. This type of information misleading has already been used by attackers to create false information. During the reports of the Parkland, Florida incident, AI-powered software was used to create fake videos and recordings of them saying misleading information. Even worse than that, researchers believe this technology will play a huge role in spreading false information during the presidential elections. Deepfakes, a company that produces AI software, allowed users with minimal technological experience to create cropped faces over people in real videos. They also have the ability to create realistic voices of celebrities. Deepfakes technology can be easily used to make political candidates look and sound like they are in compromising situations. Without thorough research being done on the video people are seeing, many people will fall victim to this type of misleading information. There are already ways to find out if a video has been made using AI technology; however, the real problem will be the belief that is created through the videos by unsuspecting viewers (Newcomb, 2018).

With all these types of attacks becoming more popular, there are ways to stop the attacks from happening. Data spoofing will be vital to protect against. A new system called a generative adversarial network (GAN) was created to help stop data spoofing. GANs are a type of AI that uses two networks that are trained on the same data. The first network analyzes the data and creates synthetic data. The other network uses the same data set to make sure the input is from a viable source. These GAN systems can be used in many different ways, but their main goal is to secure AI. By creating realistic adversarial data, these systems become very effective in the training of AI systems for defense against attacks. Ian Goodfellow, the creator of GAN systems, is hopeful that this technology was created with enough time for companies to utilize the technology and protect their AI (Snow, 2018).

Phishing attacks are already a huge problem, even before AI made the attacks better. IT security professionals will need to start better training people to spot false emails and put policies in place for training against attacks like fishing attacks. There are some new technologies that will help filter out malicious emails. Running AI within your spam filter can be one of the best ways to stop phishing. Even with this system in place, there will likely be more successful phishing attacks in the future (Jones, Groom, Groom, 2016).

Once an attacker has made its way inside a system using a phishing attack, there are ways to help detect and stop attackers. AI can also stop hackers, whether they are using AI or not, from accessing important information. Systems like Amazon's Macie are designed to be integrated within your company's network and monitor user activity. These systems store user's daily activity and put out flags to IT security teams that a security threat has been detected. The AI in place memorizes not only the path users take to access information, but it also remembers where you accessed the information. It can even get as complex as the time of day the user would normally access the information (Amazon, n.d.). For example, if a user would normally access information from their desktop but is now accessing it from a mobile device, the AI will recognize the change and set the appropriate actions in place. Depending on the threat detected, an appropriate action can be set. This action can be as little as a flag to a security administrator or as severe as shutting down a system. The AI will also make checks to make sure that information like passwords and keys are not in areas that are unsecure. If a user accidentally saves information to an incorrect area, the AI will notify the user of the mistake they made. This technology will drastically improve security within the cloud and will hopefully secure more at-home devices as well in the future (Earl, 2018).

AI can also be used to determine weak spots of security within a given network. According to a study done by chief security officer (CSO), 22% of the companies they surveyed were interested in using AI as a way to better understand the security threats that could happen within their system (Oltsik, 2018). By allowing the AI to run within your network, you are letting it detect and analyze the areas that pose security threats. Essentially, you are automating what white-hat hackers do for a living. The AI would replace white-hats and be constantly monitoring for areas of improvement. That being said, there is much more to hacking into a network than finding vulnerabilities. Hackers will often do extensive reconnaissance before ever entering a network. Hackers can often gain confidential information by simply employing a social hacking attack to try and get as much information as possible by just speaking with employees. However, with this AI monitoring security weak spots, it will still be much more difficult to enter a network without making some sort of face-to-face reconnaissance (Jones, Groom, Groom, 2016).

AI can both help and be a threat to cybersecurity. Because AI is so new, many people are still skeptical of its uses. Technology companies often feel like AI is being marketed incorrectly and it is confusing its customers. There are still many issues with this growing industry. Companies need to remember that these machines, while intelligent, are still just machines. Hackers may use these machines, but are still inherently human. Being human over a machine still has its advantages. AI does not look for signatures or calling cards that hackers use to personalize their attacks. It cannot stop an attacker that knows how to trick the AI. New training needs to be done on a consistent basis if AI security is to work properly because malware is constantly evolving. Security developers are making strong indications that AI and machine learning should not be your only way of implementing security. There will be times when your AI has not seen a specific phishing email in its training and will not know what to do. Companies are creating ways for the AI to ask for help rather than just allow or deny. The idea is that AI should be considered as an inhibitor of increased security and not the overall solution. It should help you reach your goals, not be your final goal (Newman, 2018).

AI has been developing rapidly in recent years. We have come a long way since the idea of AI. What we used to see as AI is now laughable to the capabilities we have today. AI and machine learning have both been a great success and enemy to IT security teams. AI can help companies in almost all aspects of their security strategy. You no longer need to worry about constant monitoring and looking for vulnerabilities within your network. What required specialized training can now be automated. On the other side, attacks are becoming more intelligent as well. AI can help hackers create better and smarter attacks. It can also help criminals do these attacks much quicker. The IoT is allowing AI to create new attacks through hivenets and machine-powered attacks. These attacks would normally require a human to control them, but can now be run completely by machines. Malware and other schemes are more intelligent and can take psychological factors into account when being created. The ability to poison data is becoming more popular and easier to do. It will be necessary to train human users to be better prepared for the coming attacks. However, with all of these attacks, AI will continue to grow. AI will be a great inhibitor of improvements to security and protection of online resources. Many companies are even starting to implement this technology already. The future of machine versus machine security is fast approaching, and the threats and protection against them are developing quickly.

References

Amazon. (n.d.). *Amazon Macie*. Retrieved from https://aws.amazon.com/macie/.

Anyoha, R. (2017 August 28). *The History of Artificial Intelligence*. Retrieved from http://sitn.hms.harvard.edu/flash/2017/history-artificial-intelligence/.

Drinkwater, D. (2018 January 22). *6 Ways Hackers will Use Machine Learning to Launch Attacks*. Retrieved from https://www.csoonline.com/article/3250144/machine-learning/6-ways-hackers-will-use-machine-learning-to-launch-attacks.html.

Earl, R. (2018 April 18). *Are You Sure You're Prepared for A.I. Cyberattacks?* Retrieved from https://www.atlanticbt.com/blog/malicious-ai-learn-to-hack-humans/.

Fortinet. (2017 November 17). *Fortinet Predicts Highly Destructive and Sel-Learning "Swarm" Cyberattacks*. Retrieved from https://www.fortinet.com/corporate/about-us/newsroom/press-releases/2017/predicts-self-learning-swarm-cyberattacks-2018.html.

Jones, S., Groom, F., Groom, K. (2016). *Network and Data Security for Non-Engineers*. Abington, Oxford: Taylor & Francis.

Keromytis, A., Polakis, J., Sivakorn, S. (2016). *I'm Not a Human: Breaking the Google reCAPTCHA*. Retrieved from https://www.blackhat.com/docs/asia-16/materials/asia-16-Sivakorn-Im-Not-a-Human-Breaking-the-Google-reCAPTCHA-wp.pdf.

Knight, W. (2016 December 15). *How Long Before A.I. Systems Are Hacked in Creative New Ways?* Retrieved from https://www.technologyreview.com/s/603116/how-long-before-ai-systems-are-hacked-in-creative-new-ways/.

Lord, N. (2017 March 20). *What is Polymorphic Malware? A Definition and Best Practices for Defending against Polymorphic Malware*. Retrieved from https://digitalguardian.com/blog/what-polymorphic-malware-definition-and-best-practices-defending-against-polymorphic-malware.

Newcomb, A. (2018 February 21). *Artificial Intelligence Could Supercharge Hacking and Election Meddling, Study Warns*. Retrieved from https://www.nbcnews.com/tech/innovation/artificial-intelligence-could-supercharge-hacking-election-meddling-study-warns-n849601.

Newman, L. (2018 April 29). *AI Can Help Cybersecurity-If It Can Fight through the Hype*. Retrieved from https://www.wired.com/story/ai-machine-learning-cybersecurity/.

Oltsik, J. (2018 January 25). *Artificial Intelligence and Cybersecurity: The Real Deal*. Retrieved from https://www.csoonline.com/article/3250850/security/artificial-intelligence-and-cybersecurity-the-real-deal.html.

Polyakov, A. (2018 February 20). *How AI-Driven Systems Can Be Hacked*. Retrieved from https://www.forbes.com/sites/forbestechcouncil/2018/02/20/how-ai-driven-systems-can-be-hacked/#6b33f33a79df.

Seymour, J., Tully, P. (n.d.). *Weaponizing Data Science for Social Engineering: Automated E2E Spear Phishing on Twitter*. Retrieved from https://www.blackhat.com/docs/us-16/materials/us-16-Seymour-Tully-Weaponizing-Data-Science-For-Social-Engineering-Automated-E2E-Spear-Phishing-On-Twitter-wp.pdf.

Smith, D. (2018 January 22). *How to Hack and Intelligent Machine*. Retrieved from https://www.scientificamerican.com/article/how-to-hack-an-intelligent-machine/.

Snow, J. (2018 March 27). *To Protect Artificial Intelligence from Attacks, Show it Fake Data*. Retrieved from https://www.technologyreview.com/s/610656/to-protect-artificial-intelligence-from-attacks-show-it-fake-data/.

Chapter 5

Artificial Intelligence and IT Management

Dave Pickens

Pace Harmon

Contents

General Intro

The definition of Information Technology (IT) Management varies slightly depending upon with whom you are interacting. Technopedia defines IT Management as "the process whereby all resources related to information technology are managed according to an organization's priorities and needs. Information Technology Management includes material resources like networking hardware, computers and people, as well as intangible resources like software and data. The central aim is to generate value through the use of technology". TechTarget supplies us with a more succinct definition: "IT management is the process of overseeing all matters related to information technology operations and resources within an IT organization".

The question is what can Artificial Intelligence (AI) do to help IT managers better oversee the operations and resources at hand. This chapter outlines some areas where AI is being used in IT Management today, as well as where future uses are being anticipated.

Chapter Framework

One of the major frameworks or practices used widely for IT Management is Information Technology Infrastructure Library (ITIL), and there has been a conscious effort made to organize and align this chapter with ITIL to both provide a solid outline as well as allow for easy cross-referencing. Three things you may notice immediately, however:

1. The order between Service Operations and Service Design has been swapped. This was done intentionally as there is a disproportionate deployment of AI today in the area of Operations as opposed to Design.
2. Only nine parts of ITIL are being covered: five in Service Operations and four in Service Design. Covering just nine parts is done intentionally as not all parts of ITIL are conducive to AI, let alone automation.
3. Security is absent, which is not to say that Security cannot be automated nor is it unconducive to AI deployment. Quite the opposite in fact. Security is one of the areas in which AI can be deployed heavily and have such a significant impact to the point where it should be own chapter or book.

Service Operations

Service Operations are the actual day-to-day operations involved in management of the IT environment. The goal of Service Operations is to effectively and efficiently deliver IT services. This includes things such as fixing service failures, resolving problems, fulfilling user requests, and other routine operational tasks (Kempter). Service Operations are being prioritized over Service Design because most of the AI work to date is being done in this area. The general reason why much of the AI work is done is that operating IT is labor intensive and there's a significant history of automation.

Service Operations are made up of nine processes according to the 2011 ITIL standards:

- *Event Management*
- *Incident Management*
- *Request Fulfillment*
- *Access Management*
- *Problem Management*
- *IT Operations Control*
- *Facilities Management*
- *Application Management*
- *Technical Management*

We focus specifically on five of the nine processes listed above, and they are Event Management, Incident Management, Request Fulfillment, Access Management, and Problem Management. Unfortunately, this chapter ignores Operations Control, Facilities Management, Application Management, and Technical Management – while these may be argued as having automation and AI work being done within these areas, it's either limited or highly specialized in such a way as to not be generally exposed to IT management and leadership.

General Overview of Where AI Is Making an Impact Today

AI is making an impact on at least four areas of Service Operations today (Manickavel, 2018):

- *Labor* – automating existing tasks that were previously difficult or not possible.
- *Effectiveness* – making current automations or manual tasks more effective.
- *Scheduling* – making scheduling people or tasks more accurate.
- *Speed* – reducing the time to complete an operations cycle overall.

The following sections will look across the five processes in Service Operations that we cover here (Event Management, Incident Management, Request Fulfillment, Problem Management, and Access Management), delve a little deeper into where AI is impactful, provide some examples, and present a forward outlook as to how AI might add more value.

Event Management

Event Management's role is to make sure that things, configuration items such as devices, and services are monitored continually and then filter and categorize events to decide on appropriate actions. A simple example might be monitoring filesystem free space to inform someone, most likely a storage admin, so that the person can then add capacity to the impacted filesystem before it runs out of capacity. More sophisticated Event Management environment would automate the process to eliminate as much manual effort, including mistakes, as possible through scripting and even incorporate other aspects such as prioritization (e.g., filesystem A for production is more important than filesystem B for developers) as expansion capacity is not infinite.

Where AI Is Making an Impact in Event Management Today

AI has already begun to make an impact in Event Management in at least five ways (a significant reason that AI can fit in Event Management is fuzzy matching) (Mann, 2017):

1. *Event Consolidation/Correlation*
2. *Elimination of False Positives*
3. *Thresholds*
4. *Autonomous Actions*
5. *Trend Analysis*

Event Consolidation and Correlation

Event Consolidation and Correlation are closely related. Event Consolidation is the function of reducing multiple events that are nearly identical, only allowing for small variations between the events (e.g., timestamp), down to a minimal number – ideally one. Event Correlation is the function of reducing multiple seemingly unconnected events down to a minimal number – ideally one. Correlation is seen as orders of magnitude more difficult than consolidation because it looks across what look like unrelated events all but the most experienced of administrators.

AI enhances both Consolidation and Correlation via two mechanisms:

- *Fuzzy matching* – identifies non-identical duplicates of an alert by specifying parameters to match on and threshold by which to match. Values need not be exact to find a match, and they need to fall within the user-specified or predefined parameters (e.g., if the same error message appears within 2 min of the previous one and everything matches except time/date, it is considered a duplicate).
- *Machine learning* – can build a model of what exactly constitutes a duplicate either based upon self-learning where the tool is fed a set of data without pointing out the identified duplicates to the tool or guided (supervised) learning where a dataset is fed into it that has which an experienced operator would consider duplicates. Machine learning is beneficial because often even a senior administrator can't codify precisely what the rules should be (e.g., 2 min vs. 3 min) for defining a duplicate alert or event.

Elimination of False Positives

A false positive, also called a "false alarm", is when a monitoring system generates an alert or event that indicates a given condition exists (e.g., a filesystem is running out of space) when it does not. This is a waste of resources to chase down false alarms and can also result in what is sometimes called "alarm fatigue". Alarm fatigue is the classic case of the Boy Who Cried Wolf – aka That Filesystem Is Out of Space Again – Not! We know there are always situations in every environment that the system administrators consider blips – single "out-of-space" alert because someone temporarily exceeded a threshold once while copying files. Alternatively, every third Thursday when Pete backups his laptop, AI doesn't get tired and can learn that Pete backups his laptop every third Thursday of the month and that it's always from this building and before noon. So when in November and an out-of-space alert message appears on the third Thursday but it's after 5 P.M., maybe it's a real out-of-space situation.

Thresholds

Perhaps one of the most tedious aspects to any monitoring and alert tool is to set thresholds. Whether it's the warning threshold or the error threshold, setting the threshold initially is seen as being laborious *and* tedious. This includes establishing the initial thresholds as well as sustaining, *updating*, them on an ongoing basis. Yes – they can, *and should*, change over time – no IT environment is static.

While most monitoring and alert tool providers have a default threshold based upon general practices, AI – specifically machine learning – can remove the tedious task of customizing and updating continually. Leveraging unsupervised learning, AI can adjust both the warning and error thresholds as the environment changes over time.

Autonomous Action

The ultimate goal of Event Management is to effect an outcome if needed. What this means is that the last step in the chain of an "event" would be to take an actual action (e.g., add storage to a file space). Rather than merely consolidate or correlate the alert, AI is now just beginning to offer the ability to take that final step in the process and take autonomous action. It may be as simple as executing an existing script via API (application program interface) (Janakiram, 2018).

Trend Analysis

Traditional monitoring and Event Management tools without AI almost always include some form of basic graphing and trending analysis out-of-the-box. However, conventional tools without AI don't do so well with cyclical (or periodic) trending unless explicitly configured to do so. AI-enhanced monitoring and Event Management tools can go beyond basic trending to automatically begin to look for patterns or cycles that often escape humans' view. Alternatively, in some situations, the administrators set up the non-AI-enhanced tool but simply stopped after the basic configuration step.

Let's look at some examples of where AI can make an impact in Event Monitoring. In the first example, we'll examine what happens when a server fails to say because of a faulty power supply. In the second example, we'll go back to the common situation where a filesystem is running out of space.

Example 1

Not every server has dual power supplies, and not every server with dual power supplies will stay up and running when one of them fails. So what happens when a server goes down in this case?

A FLOOD OF EVENTS!

If the underlying hardware is being monitored, an event saying "server down – power supply" is generated. The network monitoring tool then generates an event saying "network physical interface – down" for each physical network port. The network monitoring tool then generates an event saying "network – IP address unreachable" for each IP address configured on those physical network ports. The storage monitoring system may generate an event saying "server X physical connection interrupted" depending upon how the server is accessing the storage system.

The general monitoring system will likely generate an event saying "Windows OS on server X is down". The middleware monitoring system will generate an event saying "Apache 7.0 instance QA-BRFGS-Indianapolis is unreachable". The database monitoring system will say "MySQL instance QA-BRFGS-Indianapolis is unreachable". Also, in more sophisticated IT shops, they will monitor the application itself and that system will say "Application QA-BRFGS is down!"

For those of you keeping count – that's eight alerts for a single issue (power supply) in just one cycle of monitoring. Imagine if each of these conditions is being monitored every 30 s – that's 16 alerts per minute, 80 alerts in 5 min, and 240 alerts in 15 min!

An AI-based Event Management system can correlate these seemingly unrelated events through fuzzy logic as it can make a match based upon timing, location, known relationships, and so on. Ultimately concluding that until server X comes back online and is running, there is no need to get the network, middleware, database, and application administrators and technicians up in the middle of the night – just yet – as the root cause of all these alerts is the bad (failed) power supply (Soulez, 2019).

Example 2

Let's say the monitoring tool is set up to look at filesystems every 15 min. Most tools can have two thresholds set for monitoring any device or item – warning and critical. In the case of storage, the monitoring system may generate a warning alert when the filesystem reaches 70% of its allocated capacity, and it will create a critical alert when the filesystem reaches 85%.

Consider the case where a filesystem is filling up at roughly 1% per hour, and it just reached 70% of its capacity after operating acceptably for months and months.

Every 15 min now there's a warning – first four come in and say the same thing "WARNING – filesystem G on Server QA-BRFGS-Indianapolis has reached 70% capacity". Hour 2 – there are four more warnings, "WARNING – filesystem G on Server QA-BRFGS-Indianapolis has reached 71% capacity". This continues for the next 13 h until the message changes to "CRITICAL WARNING – filesystem G on Server QA-BRFGS-Indianapolis has reached a CRITICAL capacity of 85%", sometimes in the middle of the night.

An AI-enhanced monitoring and Event Management tool can do the following ("How AI Can Optimize Storage Capacity and Performance Planning"):

1. See (learn) that the capacity trend (curve) is suddenly different, and instead of just brushing off the initial WARNINGs, determine that it is more severe than usual.
2. See (learn) that the typical pattern of taking several weeks to fill up – the trend is showing that the filesystem is very likely to exceed CRITICAL levels within 15 h and fill up shortly over 24 h.
3. That adding storage space is only a short-term solution – potentially.
4. Moreover, further that the "normal" amount of capacity usually added to solve the issue might not be suitable either – e.g., need to add more capacity than the usual 10% bump until the real issue is fixed – it concluded that this 1% per hour is the "new normal".

Future Outlook for AI in Event Management

AI use in Event Management is one of the more mature areas, which is why this may be the most extended section of this chapter, because of the nature of Event Management itself. Machine learning will undoubtedly bring more sophisticated and accurate correlation which can further reduce alarms and false positives. Enhanced trend analysis will improve understanding of patterns and assist with defining what "normal" means in any given situation (e.g., what is normal Monday 8 A.M. vs. storage capacity running out).

Incident Management

The primary objective of Incident Management is to return the IT service to users as quickly as possible. To go a bit further with what is involved, it also encompasses defining and managing the entire lifecycle of all incidents. Incidents are often confused with problems – an easy way to remember is that the incident is the outage itself, whereas a problem is a cause.

Going back to the previous example of running short on storage space – running out of or having a very high degree of likelihood of running out of space on the filesystem is the incident because it will cause an interruption in service. The underlying problem was that the application suddenly began filling up the filesystem faster than normal.

Where AI Is Making an Impact in Incident Management Today

Incident Management is being enhanced in varying degrees in four ways:

1. *Notification*
2. *Collaboration*
3. *Auto-recovery*
4. *Escalation*

Notification

When an incident occurs, it's not uncommon to either fail to notify the best people to address the issue or do the exact opposite, notifying everyone "just in case". Neither is ideal, and both are inefficient. Failing to notify the correct or "best" people results in either delay getting the incident resolved or the worst case results in someone unqualified attempting to fix it. Under-notification also means that at some point, the people notified need to understand and recognize that someone else should be involved – which may or may not happen promptly.

Notifying everyone results in wasting resources (people's time) in the short term, and in long term, it can result in alarm fatigue. Over-notification means that too many people are involved of which a portion may not be able to contribute, and even if they can contribute or are knowledgeable in the area, there's a duplication of talent that is otherwise not required to address the issue at hand. Finally, over-notification can result in alarm fatigue if it happens over and over again.

Notification isn't merely a matter of identifying the right technical people who should be involved in addressing the problem but would include notifying a designated incident manager who is responsible for running/managing the Incident Management process from start to finish. Notification also goes beyond notifying the technical stakeholders and incident manager that are tasked with remedying the incident to include other stakeholder groups. These other stakeholder groups might consist of end users, application/service managers, and application/service owners that are otherwise being impacted or need to be aware of the incident.

Collaboration

One aspect of Incident Management that is closely related to the notification is collaboration. As part of best practice in Incident Management, an "incident bridge" is set up – this can range from something as simple as an audio conference bridge to the more elaborate online collaboration tools such as Skype/WebEx, and even include actual physical conference room space depending upon the nature and severity of the incident. What (and whom as outlined in the Notification section) is required is dependent upon the severity of the incident. Failure to recognize what (or whom) is required results in missteps that ultimately delay resolution of the Incident and Impact Service Availability.

Auto-Recovery and Restoration

There are situations where the solution, or at least the initial step toward a solution, is well known and should be applied before anything else. Machine learning can be based upon previous successful actions (supervised learning), once it learns from the incident that is first raised, it can perform tasks automatically and resolve the incident without any human intervention.

An excellent example of this is a simple reboot. Whether it's your PC or the server running Oracle, a simple first step seems always to be to reboot. While the sequence of steps to reboot a server or restart a database is more complicated than rebooting a PC or laptop, the general theory is very much the same. By rebooting, it clears anomalies and gets to a known (and generally good) state from which to begin any diagnostics or investigation.

Some of the more enterprise-level database products such as Oracle has offered auto-recovery capabilities enhanced by machine learning already. Oracle has added several features over the years to provide more and more granular (which means faster) auto-recovery. The most recent version of Oracle's Database product, Oracle Database 19c, introduces machine intelligence to allow the product to be highly autonomous based upon a reduced set of parameters. Oracle went as far as to extend this beyond recovery and into security which is also top-of-mind for IT ("Database New Features Guide", 2019).

Escalation

There are situations where the solution is unknown, the course of action cannot be agreed upon for one reason, or things are taking too long. That's where and when escalation becomes key. AI can add value when it comes to Incident Management escalation, and you'll see this again in Problem Management with a slightly different take.

Human administrators or technical resources are reluctant for various reasons to escalate anything. Carefully created escalation processes can ensure that unresolved problems don't linger and incidents are promptly addressed. However, even with an impartial incident manager, escalations can get delayed or the worst case completely overlooked. AI is the most useful impartial resource that can be brought to bear and can escalate by leveraging machine learning (Mann, 2018) taking into account a variety of factors such as:

- Is this an issue we've seen before or similar to something we've seen before?
- Has everyone who has been notified checked in?
- Is collaboration happening?
- Is progress being made?
- Has the clock run out?

Example

An example of where AI is making significant inroads today is auto-recovery and restoration. For a while now, Oracle has offered the ability to roll back and forward transactions. When first introduced, this required manual setup and intervention to execute. Also, as newer versions of the Oracle Database have been released, this feature has become more and more automatic extending beyond rolling transactions back and forward. More recent versions of Oracle offer the ability to recover data automatically at a very granular level from online backups or standby databases running on other servers – all without any DBA intervention required. Oracle brings some Machine Intelligence to assist DBAs in determining how many online backup copies and standby databases are necessary to meet Service Level requirements.

Future Outlook for AI in Incident Management

Because of the significant visibility of a problem when it becomes an outage, along with the labor cost to address incidents, AI has a tremendous opportunity in Incident Management across the four areas outlined above.

- *Smarter and more targeted notifications* – just the right amount at only the right time to just the right people; Incident Management tools with embedded AI will be more and more accurate on the notifications.
- *Collaboration* – going beyond the mundane such as setting up bridges but proactively pulling reports to make them readily accessible to the technical people involved of recent changes that may have had a hand in causing the incident or previous issues which may provide a clue as to the cause of the current incident.
- *Auto-recovery and restoration* – once AI becomes thoroughly entrenched and mature in auto-recovery/restoration, the push will be upstream to see if anything can be done preventatively to have avoided the problem that caused the outage in the first place.
- *Escalation* – in the future, AI will not only get better at the actual notification process itself but will also go beyond to assist in creating the escalation process, to begin with, and to update (sustain) it going forward based upon the behaviors of the people involved.

Request Fulfillment

Request Fulfillment is the process by which minor (standard) changes (e.g., requests to change a password) or requests for information are handled. For several years, there were significant efforts made to automate Request Fulfillment because it is highly labor intensive. Initial efforts started as basic "self-service" access for end users to enter requests themselves, ensuring that the appropriate information was gathered for what was being requested.

AI has already been started to be seen somewhat today in this area – primarily via the "chatbot" (Stover, 2019) or virtual request agent (Parlo, 2017). Often, this is used to direct a requestor to the proper process, provide guidance on the process itself, and even assist with initiating the process. Virtual agents often can lend assistance in the following scenarios:

- New personnel and contractors to learn how to begin a request for a specific service or items properly.
- Assist end users that infrequently request things to initiate a request.
- Assist end users with items or services that are rarely requested.

Other than assisting people as outlined above, AI is beginning to make inroads into the approvals and workflow space (Watson, 2018). One of the most significant issues with approval and workflow systems is the upkeep of the rules. In previous generations of IT Service Management (ITSM) tools, it was typical for approvals and workflow to be hardcoded in such a way that when a specific individual left or went on vacation, approvals stacked up or the workflow effectively broke.

We are just now seeing AI being leveraged to identify approval and workflow bottlenecks – learning what to do when approval queues get too full, to reroute tickets and to escalate tickets as needed ("AI Ticketing"). Additionally, there are often items or services that need to be bundled together to ensure proper functionality of the original request (e.g., prerequisites) which have different approval processes and workflows. AI is having an impact here in three ways:

1. Ensuring that all prerequisite or co-requisite items are requested as part of the initial request;
2. Looking at frequently requested items done in parallel (e.g., more storage, SharePoint access) that while not a prerequisite, enhance productivity; and
3. Setting fulfillment expectations of the requestor not only based upon all of the approvals required (e.g., more approvers = more time to fulfill request) but also based upon historical data (e.g., Steve and Dave approve typically within 24 h, but Randy takes all 3 days and then some, so if Randy is involved, make sure to set expectations correctly) (Violino, 2019).

The last step is fulfilling the request. In mature IT organizations, the final stage of fulfillment is automated to a large degree (e.g., Puppet) though not completely end to end. This is an area where AI has yet to make a significant impact.

Example 1

Properly setting expected service completion time. While a straightforward example was provided above, that only begins to scratch the surface of what is possible. Let's take a look at something more complicated.

Request for hardware and software, which requires approvals from multiple departments and even some provisioning work in SharePoint and AD to be completed. Plus, the date also needs to factor in ship date from the hardware supplier. Supervised machine learning can begin to understand and develop a model of how each of these factors influences the expected completion time ("The Future of the AI-Powered Service Desk", 2017).

For example, the AI engine learns that multiple department approvals only seem to be an influence (e.g., it makes the completion time 1.5 × longer) only when there are more than two different departments involved. Hardware delivery time is always accurate as the supplier provides with just a few outliers which can be ignored. AD and SharePoint requests are still completed within 24 h of the final department approval regardless of the day of the week so that the final rule to provide an accurate completion estimate is that it's the longer of (approval time + 24 h) or hardware delivery date as transmitted by Supplier.

Example 2

Suggested items – we've all experienced this scenario as part of online shopping. "People who buy X also have bought Y". Knowing who you are, where you work (location), who your peers are, etc. results in a better "shopping cart" experience in the Service Catalog. For example, a new hire is requesting a laptop as part of their first week on the job. The system knows that they are (1) a new hire, (2) a trainer, (3) who works from home when not traveling, (4) reports to the sales department, and (5) travels more than 50% of the time. Based upon these factors, it highlights a specific bundle of equipment that is "mandatory" and offers suggestions on other optional items that would make their travel and work-from-home experience better (Ram).

Future Outlook for AI in Request Fulfillment

In some ways, Request Fulfillment seems like it's one of the more mature areas for AI impact; however, it's not widely deployed, even though there have been demonstrable technology and multiple use cases. Personal assistants such as Siri or Alexa for business will begin to show up more and more in Request Fulfillment, simplifying the user experience and making things work (Menon, 2018).

Problem Management

The primary objectives of Problem Management are to prevent incidents from happening and to minimize the impact of incidents that cannot be prevented. Proactive Problem Management analyzes Incident Records and uses the data collected by other IT Service Management processes to identify trends or significant problems. Underlying all of this is the requirement to manage the lifecycle of all problems.

One point of confusion within IT is the difference between an incident and a problem. An incident is an outage or interruption of a service or system.

Incident Management is the process to restore the system or service. A problem is the underlying root cause of the incident, while Problem Management is the process to determine the underlying root cause of one (or more) incidents and prevent the problem from reoccurring.

AI contributes to Problem Management in three areas:

- *Escalation*
- *Correlation/Root Cause Analysis*
- *Trending/Pattern Analysis*

Escalation

Let's face it – humans are a fallible lot. Often, we overestimate our abilities, underestimate the time it will take to accomplish things, and generally muck things up if left unchecked. One aspect of both Incident Management and Problem Management that AI is helping out with is Escalation.

Escalation is easily overlooked in Problem Management because the immediacy has been removed (e.g., there is no longer an outage occurring as that's been addressed via Incident Management) and now the root cause needs to be fixed. While Escalation isn't as critical with Problem Management as it is with Incident Management, it's still vital to efficient IT management overall. If the root cause isn't addressed, the same problem keeps happening over and over again.

Correlation/Root Cause Analysis

Humans have evolved in such a way that we have learned to associate causality with correlation which isn't always the situation. Beyond assisting with escalations, AI excels at tasks such as correlation and identifying potential root causes. Exact correlation is one tool that can help in determining and locking down the root cause of a problem. Using machine learning to tackle root cause analysis is not new; it's been used in industries such as chemical, aerospace, and automotive engineering for a while now. Early adoption in these industries was possible due to the risk to life and safety if problems were solved and prevented from reoccurring. Also, since root cause analysis requires significant time, human resources, and expert knowledge when done manually, the financial value was also readily apparent. It is just recently where machine-based learning to aid root cause analysis is being used in areas such as help desk and IT Management as it has become easier and more affordable to use.

Trending/Patterns

This was fairly well covered in the Event Management section but is also a sizeable part of Problem Management and worth noting here even briefly. AI can easily go well beyond the basic correlation for the current problem at hand. It can comb through mountains of historical and seemingly non-related data. Through unsupervised machine learning, AI can identify other similar problems that could be related somehow and any underlying key influencers that were just not that obvious to a human reviewing the same data (Crittenden).

Example

Some of the more visible, and popular, consumer services include video on demand (VOD). Many of the major VOD providers leverage machine learning for correlation of data, and even root cause analysis after major outages happen. Something as seemingly small skipping a step when updating software can have a significant impact. In one case, a patch to a Java Virtual Machine (JVM) was required due to security reasons. A process was developed, documented, and scripted (automated). Because of the architecture of the VOD applications, servers can easily be taken offline, changes made and added back into the pool where work is load balanced across the servers. The script included details to take the server out of the pool, update the JVM, and add it back into the load-balancing pool.

Unfortunately, while the JVM update was applied correctly to each server, not all the servers behaved the same after the patch. While checking to see that the JVM patch was applied, it added the server back into the pool without validating the functionality of the application on each server independently. The problem was masked by the fact that some servers were working correctly which allowed for limited services. Machine learning-based root cause analysis was able to identify a pattern based solely on a tiny hardware difference between the systems that worked and those that didn't.

Future Outlook for AI in Problem Management

More and more solutions offering AI-enhanced root cause analysis will continue to come to market, whether as part of major tools like ServiceNow or otherwise – often via SaaS. These tools will be easier to use than a spreadsheet, be faster because they take advantage of affordable graphics processing units (GPUs) like NVIDIA RTX 2080 Ti, and less expensive as well.

Access Management

Access Management seems like a simple thing – granting (authorized) users the right to use a service, while preventing access to non-authorized users. The Access Management processes themselves are essentially executing policies defined in Information Security Management. Access Management is sometimes also referred to as Rights Management or Identity Management. And while closely related to security, it deserves to be incorporated here because of the impact AI has made already.

How Does AI Make an Impact on Access Management?

Simple – it's very labor intensive to grant or revoke access rights, which means it is incredibly costly and prone to significant rates of error. Put another way – labor arbitrage and quality.

Where AI Is Making an Impact on Access Management Today?

One of the significant areas in Access Management where AI is making an impact is role analytics. As touched upon before, one thing AI does well understand or develop patterns, determine correlation, and pinpoint underlying key influencers (Key Influencers Visualizations Tutorial – Power BI). AI can assist Access Management as to how to best logical group Access Rights based upon common patterns.

A significant downside to most access management systems is that you need to create roles manually or at the very best, get simplistic groupings based upon visible characteristics (job function/department) (Heather, 2017). These definitions also tend to be very static with periodic maintenance of roles being driven by the administrators as opposed to a dynamic system that continually maintains roles. Refer back the issue of setting an appropriately sustaining thresholds in Event Management.

As much of the part of Access Management as granting access is the process of revoking access and it is essential as well. Access analytics based upon recent use patterns or changes in data can be machine learning driven – continually reviewing to see who no longer needs access ("Elimity Blog – Insight in Identity and Access Management", 2018).

Most Access Management processes use a very simplistic set of rules such as "Access needs to be attested annually", which can lead to large gaps. AI can look at a broader, fuzzier set of logic and find gaps that would otherwise go unnoticed – potentially for up to a year (or more). Example – Annual attestation of required access took place yesterday, and John Smith quitted this morning which could mean his access is valid for 364 days.

AI is making both role and access analytics more dynamic, looking at access and approval patterns to keep roles always up-to-date, collapsing and simplifying roles where possible (Sailpoint, 2019).

As applications are added, AI helps ensure that they get added to the right roles. Finally, being machine driven, it can take into consideration attestation and audit requirements when creating roles (Painter, 2017). Adding to the burden of what a human administrator for Access Management would also need to consider would be additional things like separation of duties or removing the unaccessed/least-used items from within a particular role.

Example 1

Sally is a new hire in accounting team as a bookkeeper replacing Steve who moved to a position in sales within the organization. Linus, her manager, follows the process for new hires to get Sally an email account, network login, and enrolled as a member of the accounting team. Typically, the role-based Access Management system would be driven entirely, at least initially, by Sally's role of bookkeeper and therefore provide her access to the functions needed to do her primary role.

However, by understanding Sally is replacing Steve and therefore Sally (or someone) will likely need to have the access to all things in accounting department that Steve had, the AI-based Access Management can assist Linus in adding additional access for Sally making her more productive more quickly. Alternatively, it moves the access from Steve to another person, so it doesn't get overlooked.

Imagine the case where Steve is the admin for the accounting department's SharePoint site and instead of changing positions within the company, leaves the company entirely. If Linus doesn't understand that Steve's departure is creating a gap where effectively no one within the department will have admin rights to the department's SharePoint site, then how does this get addressed?

AI-based Access Management can also assist Linus in removing roles from Steve whom Sally is replacing. Steve is leaving the group, and even though he's still with the organization, shouldn't his admin role to the department's SharePoint site be removed?

Example 2

TrentCo is an organization with about 6,800 employees and has an extensive deployment of Microsoft SharePoint in their organization. Almost every organization has a SharePoint site where information is stored. Rather than manually adding the SharePoint as a request for every new employee, AI through machine learning discovers two things: (1) every employee should be added to read-only access for general corporate site on SharePoint, and (2) the default department role (e.g., accounting department employee) should include read/write access to the department SharePoint site.

Future Outlook for AI in Access Management

AI has been making minor contributions to Access Management for a while with the full potential yet to be exploited. While there is indeed room for improving the accuracy of roles, the real future of AI in Access Management lies in being able to take into account significantly larger and large quantities of data (e.g., location, time of day, machine ID) to not only improve accuracy of a role but at the same time increasing the granularity of access (Mixon, 2018).

AI for Service Design

What Is Service Design?

Service Design is the act of architecting and building the IT Services themselves. ITIL defines Service Design as identifying the requirements for any service including devising new service offerings as well as affecting changes and improvements to existing ones (Kempter and Kempter).

It's made up of 11 processes according to the 2011 ITIL standards:

- *Design Coordination*
- *Service Catalog Management*
- *Service Level Management*
- *Risk Management*
- *Capacity Management*
- *Availability Management*
- *IT Service Continuity Management*
- *Information Security Management*
- *Compliance Management*
- *Architecture Management*
- *Supplier Management*

This chapter will cover only four out of the nine processes in which AI is starting to demonstrate usefulness – Service Level Management, Capacity Management, Availability Management, and Service Continuity.

General Overview of Where AI Is Making an Impact Today

AI in Service Design is not as mature as Operations because of the nature of the work. Operations lend itself to automation, and AI is a natural extension of this work. AI's role today in Service Design is mainly pattern analysis and forecasting.

Future Prospects for AI in Service Design

Predictive assistance with Service Design – modeling "what if" scenarios based upon historical performance.

Taking into consideration all factors including the human element, Janice designed this service and historically has met design goal Service Level Agreements (SLAs) for availability, initial capacity, etc. within 3 months post-go-live; therefore, a 3-month warranty period is sufficient as part of Service Level Management.

Service Level Management

Service Level Management at the highest level is the function of negotiating SLAs with the customers and then designing services in accordance with the agreed Service Level targets. Service Level Management area is also responsible for ensuring that all Operational Level Agreements and underlying contracts are appropriate, and finally to monitor and report on the service levels.

Where AI Is Making an Impact on Service Level Management Today

As outlined in the Problem Management section, trending and forecasting tend to be thought of as linear when there can be so much more hidden in all the data collected.

One of the critical parts of Service Level Management SLA negotiation is knowing and understanding the customer's usage patterns (e.g., the second weekend of the month is completely dead for them). Understanding the usage patterns allows for things to be agreed upon such as being able to define appropriate (or best) maintenance window into the SLA as the second weekend of every month.

Often an IT Service is so complicated or has been modified over the years that it's nearly impossible to track or understand exactly what other services have an impact on it. Machine learning can correlate seemingly unrelated items when issues occur and therefore improve the understanding of precisely what depends upon what.

- Who should take the hit/blame?
- Who should get a pass/get the exclusion?
- Which things should be automatically excluded from an SLA?
- What is a "good" service level by which to measure against (aka "what is normal")?

Example 1

Today many organizations have an exemption process in place to allow for anomalies to be removed from the Service Level calculation. This process is mostly manual and is troubled with consistency across months. Although the first exemption is likely to remain a manual process, supervised machine learning opens up the possibility to bring a more consistent (and faster) approach to exceptions in the subsequent measurement period.

Example 2

Another example of where AI can make an impact in Service Level Management is making recommendations regarding exemptions – often the person making the initial determination as to what is or isn't an acceptable exemption does not have the in-depth technical knowledge in the area where the measurements are being taken. Factors such as the overall trend of the Supplier, the trend of the specific area being measured, previous and recent exemptions granted (or denied) in other areas, and past and recent exemptions granted (or denied) within the particular area being measured can all be factored in to assist the person actually making the decision.

Availability Management

Availability Management is the process that defines, analyzes, plans, measures, and improves all aspects of the availability of IT services. Availability Management is responsible for ensuring that all IT infrastructure, processes, tools, roles, etc. are appropriate for the agreed-upon availability targets.

Where AI Is Making an Impact in Availability Management Today

There are at least three aspects of Availability Management which are being aided by AI today.

1. *Single Point of Failure (SPOF) Analysis* – which will be covered in detail as part of Continuity Management
2. *Auto-scaling*
3. *Auto-recovery*

One aspect of Availability Management (and Capacity Management) is the ability to add incremental capacity automatically. However, some parts of the IT infrastructure auto-scale better and more quickly than others. AI can better establish both the high and low watermark settings as when to trigger auto-scale to add new capacity and when to turn off excess capacity, even taking into consideration the provisioning time lag of the different elements ("AI Infrastructure Planning – Galileo Performance Explorer", 2017). Think of the high and low watermark settings as slightly more advanced thresholds.

Auto-recovery is the ability to execute a series of steps to recover the service without human intervention – a more advanced version of rebooting the server as previously noted in this chapter. Rather than rebooting the whole server, for example, auto-recovery understands that it's faster to restart the application only, and then reboot the entire server if that does not address the issue. Some of the more enterprise-level database products such as Oracle offer enhanced auto-recovery capabilities enhanced by machine learning. Oracle has added several features over the years to provide more and more granular (which meant faster recovery) auto-recovery.

The most recent version of Oracle's Database product, Oracle Database 19c, introduces machine intelligence to allow the product to be highly autonomous based upon a reduced set of parameters. Oracle went as far as to extend this beyond recovery and into security which is also top-of-mind for IT (Condliffe, 2017).

Future Outlook for AI in Availability Management

Current capabilities in Availability Management focus on the day-to-day operations. Future outlook for Availability Management includes bringing these capabilities to the design aspect – being able to run "what if" scenarios and determine the impact a particular change would have in availability going forward (Edwards, 2019).

Capacity Management

Capacity Management is the process by which to ensure that the capacity of IT services and the IT infrastructure can deliver the agreed Service Level targets in a cost-effective and timely manner. Capacity Management considers all resources required to deliver the IT service, and plans for short-, medium-, and long-term business requirements. AI has already made a noticeable impact on Capacity Management in terms of scheduling resources and changes (Krazit, 2017).

Capacity Management for the human side of IT is often overlooked ("Genesys Debuts Forecasting and Scheduling Service", 2018). While large helpdesk or call centers have been using scheduling tools for years to assist with meeting the staffing requirements on any given shift, smaller shops have not been able to take advantage of these tools readily. Larger shops benefit from sample size – e.g., they have more people and more data points which provide better forecasting ability. Even when not using tools with some form of AI in them, smaller shops can now bring these capabilities to work for them because the embedded AI looks across the entire environment to determine optimal staffing requirements (Sebes, 2018). Factors such as when are the most outages experienced, when are the most incidents opened that cannot be automatically resolved, and even business cycles can now all be used to determine the best time to schedule which (and how many) resources in any given period ("Genesys Debuts Fastest, Most Accurate AI-Powered Forecasting and Scheduling Service for Better Workforce Management", 2018).

Much like the scheduling of humans, figuring out when is the optimal time in any given day, week, month, quarter, or year can pose a seemingly almost insurmountable problem in a $24 \times 7 \times 365$ IT environment. AI's ability to look across the entire environment provides a higher confidence level in determining the best time to schedule upgrades or planned outages, or add large amounts of capacity such that additional burn-in or testing is required (Hash, 2018; Llamas, 2016).

Future Outlook for AI in Capacity Management

Much like root cause analysis, the future for AI in Capacity Management is bringing these capabilities, once offered only to large organizations, to small- and medium-sized organizations.

Continuity Management

Continuity Management is the process by which risks that could seriously interrupt IT services are managed. IT Service Continuity Management (ITSCM) ensures that the IT can always deliver or provide the minimum agreed Service Levels, by reducing the risk from disaster events to an acceptable level and planning for the recovery of the services.

Where AI Is Making an Impact in Continuity Management Today

One key area of Continuity Management where AI has already made a substantial contribution is in SPOF analysis (Stacktical Team, 2017).

Today's environments are often complex where the final deliverable (service) relies upon a myriad of underlying components. Being able to quickly and accurately determine whether a SPOF exists somewhere in the underlying components is critical. Even when there isn't a SPOF, just being able to document the relationship between all the components and identify critical bottlenecks and weak points is vital. Machine learning side of AI primarily operates by creating maps of relationships – even with fuzzy logic – which to be ideal for finding SPOFs and bottlenecks.

Conclusion

AI has already made considerable headway in IT Management as outlined in this chapter but also has plenty of room to grow and improve undoubtedly. Some of the expectations for AI in IT Management include:

- *Cheaper and more accessible* – machine learning engines become more prevalent and less complicated to be incorporated by developers in their software packages.
- *Included by default and on by default* – no longer will AI be a differentiator between products as it is today, nor will it be optional; it will be the exception not to have some form included, and it will be turned on by default.

- *Easier to consume* – fewer parameters, less-guided learning will become the default.
- *More assistive* – though technically making it easier to consume, offering more AI-driven recommendations, kind of a reverse-guided learning if you would, will make usage and adoption even easier.

Resources

Call Centre Helper. "Genesys Debuts Forecasting and Scheduling Service." *Call Centre Helper*, 13 Nov. 2018, www.callcentrehelper.com/genesys-debuts-forecasting-and-scheduling-service-133917.htm.

Condliffe, Jamie. "Oracle's New Database Uses AI to Patch Itself." *MIT Technology Review*, MIT, 2 Oct. 2017, www.technologyreview.com/the-download/609026/oracles-new-database-uses-ai-to-patch-itself/.

Crittenden, Josh. "Exploring Power BI's Key Influencers." *BlueGranite*, www.blue-granite.com/blog/exploring-power-bis-key-influencers.

Edwards, John. "How AI Can Improve Network Capacity Planning." *Network World*, Network World, 5 Feb. 2019, www.networkworld.com/article/3338100/using-ai-to-improve-network-capacity-planning-what-you-need-to-know.html.

Elimity Blog. "Insight in Identity and Access Management." *Elimity*, 6 Dec. 2018, www.elimity.com/blog/the-impact-of-artificial-intelligence-on-iam.

Galileo. "AI Infrastructure Planning » Galileo Performance Explorer." Galileo Performance Explorer, Galileo, 13 Dec. 2017, galileosuite.com/solutions/ai-infrastructure-planning/.

Genesys. "Genesys Debuts Fastest, Most Accurate AI-Powered Forecasting and Scheduling Service for Better Workforce Management." *PR Newswire*, Genesys, 30 Oct. 2018, www.prnewswire.com/news-releases/industry-first-genesys-debuts-fastest-most-accurate-ai-powered-forecasting-and-scheduling-service-for-better-workforce-management-300739998.html.

Hash, Susan. "How AI Will Change the Nature of Contact Center Work." *Contact Center Pipeline Blog*, Contact Center Pipeline, 13 Nov. 2018, blog.contactcenterpipeline.com/2018/11/how-ai-will-change-the-nature-of-contact-center-work/.

Heather, Andy. "Applying AI to Access Management." *Information Security Buzz*, 30 Mar. 2017, www.informationsecuritybuzz.com/articles/applying-ai-access-management/.

Janakiram, MSV. "5 Ways AIOps Will Influence Enterprise IT Operations." *Forbes*, Forbes Magazine, 7 July 2018, www.forbes.com/sites/janakirammsv/2018/07/06/5-ways-aiops-will-influence-enterprise-it-operations/#430038b62672.

Kempter, Stefan and Andrea Kempter. "ITIL Service Design | IT Process Wiki." *IT Process Wiki - the ITIL® Wiki*, wiki.en.it-processmaps.com/index.php/ITIL_Service_Design.

Kempter, Stefan. "ITIL Service Operation | IT Process Wiki." *IT Process Wiki - the ITIL® Wiki*, wiki.en.it-processmaps.com/index.php/ITIL_Service_Operation.

Krazit, Tom. "How Amazon Web Services Uses Machine Learning to Make Capacity Planning Decisions." *GeekWire*, 19 May 2017, www.geekwire.com/2017/amazon-web-services-uses-machine-learning-make-capacity-planning-decisions/.

Llamas, Ramón Medrano. "Capacity Planning at Scale – Google AI." *Google AI*, Google, 13 July 2016, ai.google/research/pubs/pub45902.

Manickavel, Ramesh. "Artificial Intelligence in Service Desks - DZone AI." *Dzone.com*, 18 Oct. 2018, dzone.com/articles/artificial-intelligence-in-service-desk.

Mann, Stephen. "5 Use Cases for AI on the IT Service Desk." *IT Service Management (ITSM) Software for the Intelligent Enterprise*, 10 July 2017, www.sunviewsoftware. .com/blog/5-use-cases-for-ai-on-the-it-service-desk.

Mann, Stephen. "10 Automation and AI Tips for Working Smarter on the IT Service Desk." *ITSM.tools*, ITSM.tools, 29 Sept. 2018, itsm.tools/2018/05/01/10-automation-ai-tips-for-working-smarter-on-the-it-service-desk/.

McManus, Chris. "The Future of the AI-Powered Service Desk." *TechnologyAdvice*, 20 Dec. 2017, technologyadvice.com/blog/information-technology/future-ai-powered-service-desk/.

Menon, Ram. "Conversational AI Is Coming To The Service Desk." *Forbes*, Forbes Magazine, 27 July 2018, www.forbes.com/sites/forbestechcouncil/2018/07/27/conversational-ai-is-coming-to-the-service-desk/#4616767b2ce4.

Microsoft. "Key Influencers Visualizations Tutorial - Power BI." *s Tutorial - Power BI | Microsoft Docs*, Microsoft, https://docs.microsoft.com/en-us/power-bi/visuals/power-bi-visualization-influencers.

Mixon, Erica. "Identity and Access Management Tools Add AI, Microservices." *SearchMobileComputing*, 28 May 2018, searchmobilecomputing.techtarget.com/news/252441320/Identity-and-access-management-tools-add-AI-microservices.

Oracle. "Database New Features Guide." *Oracle Help Center*, Oracle, 13 Feb. 2019, docs.oracle.com/en/database/oracle/oracle-database/19/newft/new-features.html#GUID-E2F2E0EE-D58B-4F9C-A7F8-301D9AEA34D8.

Painter, Lee. "Could AI Improve Identity Management and Security?" *Digital Catapult - Home*, 25 Mar. 2017, www.digicatapult.org.uk/news-and-views/blog/could-ai-improve-identity-management-and-security/.

Parlo. "The 3 Essentials of AI Bots for IT Help Desk." *Chatbots Magazine*, Chatbots Magazine, 19 Dec. 2017, chatbotsmagazine.com/the-3-essentials-of-ai-bots-for-it-help-desk-9bce2ffa4446.

Rahi Systems. "How AI Can Optimize Storage Capacity and Performance Planning." *Data Center Solutions Provider*, www.rahisystems.com/blog/how-ai-can-optimize-storage-capacity-and-performance-planning/.

Ram, Ashwin. "AI in ITSM: How AI Can Make Your IT Service Desk Great." *AI in ITSM: How AI Can Make Your IT Service Desk Great*, Manage Engine, www.manageengine.com/products/service-desk/how-ai-impact-it-service-desk.html.

SailPoint. "The Machine Behind Identity Governance." *SailPoint*, 19 Feb. 2019, www.sailpoint.com/blog/machine-learning-identity-governance/.

Sebes, Christopher. "How Artificial Intelligence Is Reshaping the Restaurant World." *QSR Magazine*, QSR, 21 Dec. 2018, www.qsrmagazine.com/outside-insights/how-artificial-intelligence-reshaping-restaurant-world.

Soulez, Thomas. "How Artificial Intelligence in the Contact Center Will Work." *Nexmo*, 8 Jan. 2019, www.nexmo.com/blog/2017/03/29/artificial-intelligence-contact-center/.

Stacktical Team. "Reinventing Capacity Planning with Predictive Analytics & AI." *Medium*, Medium, 11 Feb. 2017, medium.com/@stacktical/reinventing-capacity-planning-with-predictive-analytics-ai-ad8466613aaf.

Stover, Steve. "Transforming the Service Desk: Adding AI to the Team." *CMSWire.com*, CMSWire.com, 22 Feb. 2019, www.cmswire.com/digital-workplace/transforming-the-service-desk-adding-ai-to-the-team/.

Violino, Bob. "How AI Is Helping the Help Desk." *Computerworld*, Computerworld, 8 Apr. 2019, www.computerworld.com/article/3384698/artificial-intelligence-helping-help-desk.html.

Watson, Charles. "How to Take Advantage of Artificial Intelligence in Your Contact Center." *Contact Center and Workforce Management Blog*, Injixo, 20 Sep. 2018, blog.injixo.com/workforce-management/how-to-take-advantage-of-artificial-intelligence-in-your-contact-center.

Zendesk. "AI Ticketing." *Zendesk*, www.zendesk.com/support/features/ai-ticketing/.

Chapter 6

Artificial Intelligence in Marketing

Joe Ciuffo

Genesys

Contents

"Marketing itself is a vague term that is poorly understood even by so-called professionals and experts in the industry", Allan Dib said, "it's as simple as that – marketing is the strategy you use for getting your ideal target market to know you, like you and trust you enough to become a customer". In his text, *1-Page Marketing Plan*, he clarifies no one will know that a product or a service is good unless they've made a purchase (Dib, 2018). A great product may retain customers, but expecting quality alone to lure in prospective buyers is dangerous. As a consumer, you're most likely familiar with the iPod, Blu-Ray DVD, and Kindle. But have you heard of the Microsoft Zune, HD-DVD, and Barnes & Noble Nook? The second list represents failed products that were not just competitors to the products in the first list, but even superior to their counterparts in certain aspects. Yet, they failed. Lacking a defined target market and clear messaging takes away the power to leverage a good product or service as a customer retention tool (Great Products, 2018). In a global economy with companies competing fiercely on price and features, marketing is essential to both gain the attention of an increasingly distracted consumer and differentiate among the competition. Artificial intelligence (AI) is supercharging the capabilities marketers have to reach an audience and refine their messaging.

Marketing is intended to take customer through a journey. If executed successfully, in the journey, the customer travels from the beginning to the end of the buying process; from prospect, to a lead and finally a customer. This overarching journey constitutes many divisions within marketing such as product positioning, lead generation, content marketing, and sales enablement (Dib, 2018). Each of these relies on accuracy by hitting their target audience, and self-reflection of how to improve that accuracy. When striving to resonate within a defined target, imagine a person playing the game of darts. The objective is to hit the bullseye, at the center of the dartboard, with the dart itself. Much like darts, companies are just attempting to hit their bullseye. This is done through marketing campaigns, which represent the efforts taken specifically to increase interaction with an audience and, by extension, generate revenue. The campaign is designed to have maximum potency with those expected to be interested in the product. However, without actionable data regarding the performance of a marketing campaign, the organization cannot fully understand their success (Williams, 2017). Would someone really want to play competitive darts with their eyes closed? Assuming the person is not capable of super-human feats, they would ideally want to gauge their next throw based upon the result of their first attempt. In marketing, a company collects data on the effectiveness of their campaign to then judge how they will attempt the next. Failure to improve upon marketing campaigns could result in wasted resources, and potential failure as an organization (Dopson, 2019).

Unfortunately, marketing is difficult. Companies are faced with more ways than ever to reach their audience and endless amounts of data to analyze the potency of their message. Identifying the best way to reach an audience and learning from data is not impossible, but it is time-consuming and expensive (Dib, 2018). The infusion of AI into marketing, more specifically the use of machine learning, wields abundant but time-consuming commodities, like data and channels to reach the customer, into actionable next steps. In short, AI can dramatically decrease the time of analysis and provide curated next steps for each person and unique situation. This text will review the areas of marketing evolving through the use of AI and provide examples of those utilizing this technology right now.

"Marketers need to deliver the right message, to the right customer, at the right time", Philip Kushmaro said, "and they can accomplish this with customer segmentation". The increase in data and amounts of channels to reach a prospective customer has raised the expectation of personalized marketing through customer segmentation. How can organizations leverage data to understand who they are interacting with and dynamically respond with personalized content? Machine learning, or AI, is uniquely positioned to take advantage of this problem. While segmentation is typically done through demographics, AI can go even further by identifying similar personas or characters among customer groups. "Most companies view segmentation as a method of clustering similar customers together at a given point in time. Imagine harnessing the power of AI to map the journey that each customer has taken to reach his or her present segment", said Pini Yakuel,

CEO of Optimove. "By analyzing customers based on their movement among segments over time, we can achieve dynamic micro-segmentation, and predict future behavior in a very accurate fashion. This approach can take customer segmentation to a whole new level. Using micro-segmentation, brands can communicate 'personally' with every customer, optimizing customer experience and increasing loyalty and lifetime value, in today's highly-competitive direct-to-consumer space" (Kushmaro, 2018).

Elevating customer segmentation to a personal level is a radical improvement. Historically, companies would launch and manage a few marketing campaigns at one time, each focused on a target audience. Limiting campaigns is a human restriction, not a machine one. Using data to create groupings of similar people helps identify trends and is a necessity to create next steps with the marketing data. For example, understanding how males between the ages of 18 and 35 from New Jersey shop for clothes will identify certain characteristics to emphasize in a marketing campaign. AI, more specifically machine learning, enables a unique campaign for each person the company reaches. "In other words, instead of a single nurture campaign for a million people, you launch a million campaigns", David Gutelius said, "each of which is learning from all the others, all the time" (Gutelius, 2017). Returning to our male clothing example, it's now possible to curate marketing material specific to the clothing preferences of one particular person, instead of relying on demographical data to give general insight due to lack of user-specific data.

AI powering customer personalization may seem farfetched, but many service-based companies are using this now. Organizations like Netflix, Amazon, and Yelp have relied on sophisticated machine learning to improve the customer experience through curated content. Users are prompted with movies based on their interest, notified when exciting products they might buy are available, even a reminder that it might be time to purchase more of their preferred toothpaste, and alerted when a restaurant of their palate is close by. Personalizing the experience to the specific user increases the likelihood of higher usage, lower customer churn, and potential for revenue generation. While one person may relate to Netflix as a great place to watch their favorite horror movies, another may think of it as their one-stop service for documentaries. Netflix is still the exact same service, with the same library of content, but the presentation layer or user interface is drastically altered in reaction to the user. The data doesn't have to originate within the application of use. In fact, West Elm leverages technology that ingests a customer's Pinterest data to learn and suggests household furniture and other home décor. To fully understand the impact of AI on the user experience, consider your local grocery store reorganizing the entire isle structure based on your shopping habits. It would be a monumental task; one that AI can do for every digital user in real time (Yao et al., 2018).

The benefits of automation tools increase over time, as companies analyze the performance of interactions. Did a prospect never open an email sent, or unsubscribe from text messages? These responses are acknowledged in real time, and new approaches are used to see which actions are generating positive outcomes as opposed to frustrating would-be customers with spam. The technology enables marketers to constantly learn and refine their methods immediately, not retroactively; better understanding each person within the targeted audience. Continuous improvement of marketing automation is key to nurturing prospects. Overloading a person with too many emails and information could cause frustration. However, sending just the right amount or inviting them to informational webinars can foster trust and build a long-lasting business relationship (Coveney, 2017).

Hyper-personalized marketing is important because it increases the chances of a prospect achieving a business goal. Put simply, getting someone to do what the marketing team wants is called a conversion rate. Depending on the goal, a conversion rate could be making a purchase, submitting a form, engaging in a chat with lead generation, or signing up for a newsletter. Conversion rates are tracked in a variety of marketing campaigns, such as call to action banners within promotional emails or website landing pages. Marketers strive to clearly communicate the organization's value proposition and even try different versions to test effectiveness (Andrus, 2018). But without AI, results are lackluster in their current state. According to HubSpot, roughly 22% of businesses are happy with their conversion rates. Even more important, 90% of prospective searchers stated that they haven't made their mind up about a brand before starting their search. A large gap exists between companies successfully converting potential prospects to customers and customers whose decision remains malleable (HubSpot, 2018). In a 2016 marketing study, the average conversion rate ranged from 2% to 9% depending on the industry (Rivard, 2016). We're left with a world that spends over 200 billion dollars in digital advertising, another 77 billion to convert the prospects to customers, and a paltry success rate for all this effort (Ryan, 2019).

AI-powered technologies, like the Irish start-up Altocloud, address this gap through the use of real-time customer journey shaping. Customer journey shaping is the ability to change individual experiences in real time by leveraging machine learning in response to the individual's action. As an example, imagine someone browsing a travel website and they've visited a section for Punta Cana before, in previous visits. The travel website leverages trackers that assign a unique ID to this person; collecting information such as time on website, locations, and dates most frequently searched. The users past browsing habits on the site will influence the content presented to them. On the user's visit, all of the upcoming deals on the website might only show Punta Cana and advertise a special pricing that *just so happens* to be the same dates the user has previously searched. If this person were to navigate away, abandoning their travel search, then follow-up communication could be sent via email, SMS, or the most preferred channel by the customer (Smyth & Dabrowski, 2018). The travel company might also integrate this data with social media platforms; paying to advertise Punta Cana vacations to this specific user on Facebook or Instagram (Bonometti, 2012). To tie that all together, a user's browsing history for a potential vacation has drastically altered the content a travel website displays on their main page and the advertising presented on other platforms, like social media. The travel company didn't have to create generic ads, because the user's browsing history and real-time responses told them exactly what they needed to know. These ads, directed toward potential customers with extreme precision, have the potential to increase the company's return on advertising investment.

Personalized customer segmentation is important to the travel site scenario because businesses are understanding customers at scale. Through data collection, an organization can capture the journey or paths of every successful and unsuccessful purchase. Using machine learning, we can identify patterns and customer groupings, or similarity, that correlate to a defined business goal, like purchasing vacation packages. The system identifies patterns that humans might have missed and automates the process to enable a deep understanding of data that would not have been financially possible without machine learning. If this person was initially brought in as a lead via promotional email, what should happen on the website to provide the highest likelihood that the visit ends in a booked trip? If that customer abandons the website, or items in their shopping cart, what next steps can be automated to increase chances of a return visit and again, a successful booked trip? In this situation, machine learning combines demographical data, and persona generated data from the customer's journey to predict when to engage the customer with content; like a pop-up offer, or promotional email. The system is responding to customer actions in real time and learns when actions are becoming ineffective. A certain demographic of potential summer-trip package buyers may be more receptive to *hot deal* campaigns via SMS instead of email. In this unique situation, those prospects should receive content formatted for text sent in a text message (Smyth & Dabrowski, 2018).

In *Applied Artificial Intelligence: A Handbook for Business Leaders*, Patrick Hebron noted, "Tools are not meant to make our lives easier. They are meant to give us leverage so that we can push harder. Tools lift rocks. People build cathedrals". AI enables marketers to do more. Consider the influence of AI in marketing as the difference between a musket and a modern sniper-rifle; both are guns, but one of them is a significant advancement in ability and accuracy. Just like Patrick's quote, and the comparison between the guns, marketers have the tools to be more able and precise than ever before. However, rocks are not choosing to become cathedrals and guns are not choosing where to shoot. Organizations must identify how to leverage AI to achieve their business outcomes (Yao et al., 2018). The orchestration of AI in the overall marketing strategy is still very much human. What is clear is that humans are freed to work on more impactful by automating repetitive operations and data analysis. Marketers will use this enhanced ability to supercharge business outcomes and pinpoint the correct audience with a tailored message.

References

Andrus, A. (2018, January 17). What is Conversion Rate? How to Calculate and Improve Your Conversion Rate. Retrieved from www.disruptiveadvertising.com/conversion-rate-optimization/conversion-rate/.

Bonometti, R.J. (2012, July 1). Technology Considerations for Competing in the "Big Data"-Social-Mobile-Cloud Marketing Space. Competition Forum. Retrieved from https://core.ac.uk/download/pdf/46603970.pdf.

Coveney, J. (2017, March 11). What is Marketing Automation? 21 Pros Weigh in. Retrieved March 12, 2017, from http://revenginemarketing.com/blog/what-is-marketing-automation-top-answers-from-industry-thought-leaders/.

Dib, A. (2018). *The 1-Page Marketing Plan: Get New Customers, Make More Money, and Stand Out from the Crowd.* Miami, FL: Successwise.

Dopson, E. (2019, May 16). Retargeting 101: Why It's Essential for Any Marketing Funnel. Retrieved from https://www.singlegrain.com/marketing-funnels/why-retargeting-is-absolutely-essential-for-any-marketing-funnel/.

Great Products that Failed Because of Poor Marketing. (2018, February 15). Retrieved from https://capitalandgrowth.org/articles/866/great-products-that-failed-because-of-poor-marketi.html.

Gutelius, D. (2017, January 26). Intelligence As Its Core: What Happens When AI Drives Marketing. Retrieved from https://medium.com/aimarketingassociation/intelligence-as-its-core-what-happens-when-ai-drives-marketing-5d1392e7c5e9.

HubSpot. (2018). The Ultimate List of Marketing Statistics for 2018. Retrieved from www.hubspot.com/marketing-statistics.

Kushmaro, P., & IDG Contributor Network. (2018, September 04). How AI is Reshaping Marketing. Retrieved from www.cio.com/article/3302739/marketing-industry/how-ai-is-reshaping-marketing.html.

Rivard, J. (2016, December 09). Are Your Lead Conversion Rates Above Average? Retrieved from https://marketinginsidergroup.com/content-marketing/lead-conversion-rates-average/.

Ryan, J. (2019, January 17). US B2B Digital Advertising Trends. Retrieved from www.emarketer.com/content/us-b2b-digital-advertising-trends.

Smyth, J., & Dabrowski, M. (2018, February). Analyzing and Shaping Customer Journeys [Web log post]. Retrieved from https://genbin.genesys.com/media/Analyzing-and-shaping-Customer-journeys-WP-EN.pdf.

Williams, J. (2017, May 15). What is a Marketing Campaign Anyway? – Hacker Noon. Retrieved from https://hackernoon.com/what-is-a-marketing-campaign-anyway-2d515e65367f/.

Yao, M., Jia, M., Zhou, A., & Zhang, N. (2018). *Applied Artificial Intelligence: A Handbook for Business Leaders.* Middletown, DE: TOPBOTS.

Chapter 7

Artificial Intelligence in Cloud Marketing

Lauren Donahue and Fatemeh Hajizadeh
Lev+

Contents

The Role of AI in Marketing

How Marketers Use AI

Companies are rapidly expanding their investments in artificial intelligence (AI) as it begins to play a larger role in marketing strategies. Companies like IBM, Salesforce, and Oracle all have products that utilize the technology, and 83% of companies with 1,000 or more employees planned to use AI in 2017 (Benes, 2018). Marketers utilize AI to accomplish a wide range of strategies.

Content Marketing

One of the most prominent strategies marketers use is content marketing, a tactic that focuses on creating engaging content instead of simply highlighting a specific product or promotion. By utilizing content marketing, marketers focus on building stronger relationships with their consumers (Plessis, 2017). Marketers are finding unique ways to utilize AI to improve their content marketing strategies. For example, AI can be used to evaluate success rates of digital content and update that content. If a piece of digital content is perceived with negative customer feedback, AI techniques can be utilized to update that content to become more appealing to consumers. In the same way, if content is perceived more positively, it can be updated to adapt more easily in different browsers. The artificial techniques that are responsible for this "self-learning" content can be a combination of mechanisms such as artificial neural networks or machine learning techniques (Kose, 2016). By updating content based on how users are engaging with it, AI allows marketers to provide a better user experience for their consumers.

Email Marketing

AI has also become a major player in email marketing. Salesforce is one of the companies that provides email marketers the tools to utilize AI technologies in email campaigns. In Marketing Cloud, one of the many products in the Salesforce suite, AI goes by the name of Einstein and provides a number of ways to use the technology to personalize email campaigns. In order to use this effectively, Einstein uses a combination of rule types and recommendation scenarios to predict the content that should be shown. A number of data points must be configured within the account, such as SKUs (stock keeping units) and product codes, in order for the software to know what products it can recommend. Recommendation scenarios can then be configured to display content based on how users have interacted with similar content. For example, with the "Bought Bought"' recommendation scenario, Einstein shows content based on the interactions of other customers – those who bought item x also bought item y. To enhance the user experience, waterfall predictions can be enabled. This allows the user to set the priorities of these recommendation scenarios and make the correct number of recommendations based on which is most relevant to the customer (Salesforce: Trailblazer Community).

By using AI to create intelligent recommendations for consumers based on similar behaviors, email marketers have the ability to personalize experiences and enhance the customer journey. This plays an important role in determining whether or not investment in AI technologies is worth the risk. Fifty-nine percent of shoppers feel they were influenced to make a purchase based on the fact that their interactions with a brand felt personalized to them (Infosys, 2013). This means that adding these techniques that allow for personalization, marketers can create a greater return on their investment.

Chatbots

Chatbots, or conversation agents, are not a new concept. In fact, the first ever chatbot, called ELIZA, was built and studied in 1966 by Joseph Weizenbaum at Massachusetts Institute of Technology (MIT). ELIZA was a machine used for identification of keywords, minimal context, and generation of responses using ELIZA "scripts" to perform conversational interactions with a user (Weizenbaum, 1966). Although ELIZA used much simpler technology to perform these interactions, Weizenbaum's machine laid the foundation for the utilization of similar machines to solve unique business problems.

A majority of modern chatbots use AIML, also known as artificial intelligence markup language. AIML is the foundation on which most online chatbots function, due to the fact that they are simple to configure (Satu, 2015).

While opinions are varied whether or not chatbots provide the best user experience, it has been proven that chatbots can increase engagement and provide unique business insights. For example, in the academic year (AY) of 2016–2017, Georgia State University instituted a chatbot that students could text to get information regarding pre-enrollment tasks they needed to accomplish. By instituting this chatbot, the university saw an increase of 116 more students than average following through from acceptance to matriculation. This system allowed students to receive responses to questions at any time without waiting to schedule an appointment or call an overloaded administrator during business hours. Upon the success of this project, more staff were hired to monitor the system and other universities followed suit with similar chatbot systems of their own (Bendici, 2018).

Chatbots are becoming more humanistic and more user-friendly in the process. While chatbots are predicted to handle the majority of all customer-service interactions by 2020, they currently handle 30%. The institution of chatbots is also predicted to cut annual costs for businesses by $8 billion in 2020 (Preimesberger, 2018).

Search Engine Optimization

AI is still relatively new in the realm of search engine optimization (SEO), but AI technologies are already impacting SEO today. Google has integrated AI to help process its search results in a way that is more relevant to the user. In 2015, the company released its use of RankBrain to enhance its search processes. RankBrain is a machine learning AI system that drives better search results for ambiguous search queries. Its main purpose is to drive better search results for queries that have never been searched before. On average, this equates to about 15% of all Google searches in a day (Schachinger, 2017).

Because the algorithm that Google uses is a company secret and cannot be disclosed to the public, it is extremely difficult to utilize AI to improve SEO. Researchers are beginning to anticipate how they can utilize AI to improve SEO. There are academic theories and commercial products that aim to do so. One of these academic theories is called Polidoxa, a social platform which utilizes "swarm intelligence", which in nature refers to a mass of individuals completing simple tasks to collectively complete a complex task (similar to ants building an ant hill) (Hinchey, 2007). This research attempts to provide a solution that combats the pitfalls of current search engines and social networks and combine them into an optimal solution. Polidoxa is a platform that combines social networks and search engine algorithms to shorten the length of time it takes for a page to acquire "authority" based on the trusted contacts of a user. This platform aims to give users a platform that allows them to truly understand the way their searches are filtered but utilize critical thinking to make decisions regarding their results (Biselli, 2012).

There are also commercial products currently on the market that utilize AI technologies. IBM has produced an AI solution to improve SEO through a product called SPSS Clementine. It is a data-mining product that produces web analytics modules for a number of areas, including SEO. This allows an SEO analyst to assess a company's marketing campaigns and use the data to obtain higher positions in search queries (Segall, 2009).

Despite its dormancy in SEO optimization, many SEO experts praise AI and its ability to optimize website traffic. In 2017, a study from the SEO Proficiency in Marketing Survey showed that 96% of SEO experts believe that strategies can greatly benefit from using AI and 61% agreed that AI can be used to locate strategy anomalies and correct them (Sullivan, 2017).

Why AI Is Crucial in the Digital Marketing Age

Automating Processes

Think back to the chatbot Georgia State University implemented. During its busiest application period, administrators were unburdened with calls from students seeking information they needed to prepare for the upcoming semester. By automating these communications, students were able to get the answers they needed at any time of the day and administrators had less calls to monitor. This led to an increase in the average of committed students for the year.

AI is just one of the technologies that can increase the impact of automating processes, and automations can have a substantial impact on businesses. By utilizing automated processes, companies have the ability to advance their current performance, minimize mistakes, and even potentially achieve tasks that go beyond human abilities (Yuniarthe, 2017). Many business leaders believe that automation could drastically save time and revenue they are currently investing in their business. According to WorkMarket's "2020 In(Sight) Report: What AI and Automation Really Mean for Work", 78% of business leaders believe that automation could save 360 work hours a year (WorkMarket, 2017).

Customer Connections

As discussed previously in this chapter, AI has the power to create personalized communications and increase the user experience. Consumers are slowly anticipating that brands anticipate their needs and are developing stronger brand loyalties to those that engage in personalization efforts. Ninety-one percent of consumers are more likely to shop with brands that remember their previous interactions with the brand and make relevant recommendations based on their past behavior (Accenture, 2018).

Providing personalized experiences is becoming crucial in digital marketing efforts, and marketers are actively adapting their channels to reflect that. In 2018, personalization was utilized by marketers in 77% of email communications, 52% in websites, and 31% in mobile applications (Statista, 2019).

Economic Impact

The utilization of AI has a major impact on revenue streams. This is largely due to the way businesses are analyzing customer data. As we've seen in this chapter, AI has the ability to provide increased value on customer data. In 2018, 70% of companies that utilized more than 75% of their customer data exceeded their revenue goals as opposed to the 50% who used less than that amount (Brown, 2018).

Automation also has the ability to dramatically increase marketing return on investment (ROI). Chatbots play a large role in reducing marketing costs. Currently, chatbots are estimated to be saving businesses $6 billion in customer service and marketing, and are predicted to save 2.5 billion work hours by 2023 (Alaimo, 2018). Marketing automations are not limited to chatbots. Email campaigns, mobile communications, and data migrations all have the ability to be automated as well. Twenty-eight percent of marketers report that marketing automation contributed to an increase in revenue per sale (27% of those that utilize marketing automation do not have an effective method to measure this) (Lenskold Group, 2012). As AI becomes more easily integrated into marketing automation processes, marketers will see continue to their investment in marketing create stronger returns.

Where Marketers Can Fall Short

Data

One of the major pitfalls marketers can fall into is utilizing stale, or outdated, data. With the massive amounts of data that are being collected by businesses every day, it becomes increasingly important to know where and how data is collected, what that data means for the business, and how to analyze the most effective use of that data. When data is inaccurate or outdated, AI technologies become almost useless. For example, IBM started a promotion using Watson, a machine learning product produced by the company, that would utilize AI to begin seeking stronger recommendations for treating cancer. IBM aimed to sell Watson to cancer-treating doctors, but investigation found it was unable to even learn about basic forms of cancer. One of the major reasons for the machine's errors was due to its collection of data. Much of the data collected was in the form of handwritten notes, ambiguous acronyms, and different styles of writing (Ross, 2017). This ambitious project failed due in major part to its lack of reliable and effective data.

Unreliable and bad data has already taken a major financial toll on companies in the United States. It is estimated that bad data quality costs companies in the U.S. $3.1 trillion (Redman, 2016). The reason that bad data costs so much is largely due to the amount of time and resources it takes to either recover or work around these data pitfalls. As companies begin to collect more data about their customers, it is important to have an in-depth understanding of the data that is being used and processes that can be applied to audit and validate data.

Privacy and Data Security

As marketers begin to use AI to collect data about their customers, it becomes increasingly important to remain compliant with data regulations. The implementation of the general data protection regulation (GDPR) in the EU has had a massive impact on the way companies are analyzing their data and collection processes. While the legislation aims to provide consumers control over the data companies are collecting about them, the ambiguities in the legislation make it difficult to interpret how it directly impacts AI. For example, Article 22 of the GDPR states that consumers are "not to be subject to a decision based solely on automated processing, including profiling". The power of AI relies solely on data collection by automated processes. However, this article relies on a decision being made for the automated collection of data which produces legal impacts or similarly impacts the subject of data. This leaves a lot of room for open interpretation regarding automated data collection (Spyridaki).

While the GDPR does not necessarily restrict the use of AI, it does promote ethical and intentional use of the technology. It aims to provide an environment where companies are making a constant effort to maintain trust with their customers.

The GDPR and other potential future data regulations in the U.S. may have a major impact on the way marketers are able to collect data about their consumers using AI. Now more than ever, it is important for companies to be intentional in the methods they are using to collect data and understand how the data may be used to benefit the company and its customers. It is also important to have legal teams on board that understand the complex technologies that may be implemented and how they will need to interpret these regulations in a potential lawsuit.

How AI Is Implemented in Marketing

Now that the importance of AI in marketing is more clear, understanding how it is being used by marketer and what are the essential parts of a successful marketing comes next.

Data Source and Types

One might ask where does the data for use in marketing all come from? What is a third-party data? Understanding where your data is coming from and how you can use it is an important part of marketing. It is important to understand the different types of data. Without the data, you won't be able to have a successful marketing. Depending on the situation and what marketers want to do with the data, one type will have more benefit over another (Lotame, 2018).

First-Party Data

This type of data is what a marketer collects using different channels of communication. Collection can happen on the company's website using a signup form, or it can be a lead capture form in social networks, or it can be directly from the customer relationship management (CRM) system. Because of the nature of first-party data and how it is collected, it is considered the most useful data when it comes to a successful marketing. It is the most cost-effective, clean, and relatable consumer data a marketer can have access to. The minimal privacy policy challenges involvement in this type of data increases the value of it. The high quality of first-party data will make it easier to find different options for use in marketing efforts (Lotame, 2018).

By placing tracking pixels on the website, data about the known and unknown consumers can be gathered and used to personalize the experience by the use of AI. All the information and data gathered can be placed in a centralized location such as data management preview (DMP) and be used for targeting different segments of audiences or understanding the behavior of consumers to improve the experience (Lotame, 2018).

Second-Party Data

Second-party data is a newer concept. This is a data that marketers buy from another company and it is that company's first-party data. Due to the nature of this data being the first-party data of another company, the usage and benefits of this data are the same as those of the first-party data. In addition to these benefits, this data will help you expand your network easier (Lotame, 2018).

Third-Party Data

Aggregated data coming from other resources is considered third party. It is basically a collector of data that pays others for their first-party data. Data will be aggregated and grouped into different categories based on industry, users behavior, demographic such as age and gender. The categories of data then will be broken into segments that marketers will purchase depending on their needs. It is important to understand that the same set of data is available to competitors (Lotame, 2018).

Social Networks

Advertisement in social networks such as Facebook, Instagram, and Twitter can be used to collect prospects or target audiences with personalized ads. The use of first-party anonymous tracking data or second-party data will help capturing new prospects.

Lookalike audience is a concept that is being used in platforms like Facebook, using the existing audiences from the database and creating a segment, an ad can be targeted to a lookalike audience in Facebook for capturing more leads that follow the same traits as your existing customers. Using lookalike audience has proven success for many marketers with a low cost per click. An important aspect that need to be considered when creating the audiences is that it is better to use a data with more accuracy to import to your Facebook Business Manager (Miller, 2018).

How Data Is Being Used

Machine learning is a method of data analysis and it is using the concept that machine can learn by looking at the data. Machine will find patterns in the data and makes relevant decisions. If a consumer goes to a car dealership and buys a new car, based on the data collected from the other buyers and their buying behaviors, machine can predict whether this specific person will be in the market for buying a new car in 5 years. By knowing this information, marketer can target buyers with this persona, and using the data from the past purchases, recommend the best match.

Recommendations Engine

Having access to different type of data gathered from website visits, social network engagement, email engagement, and sales can help increase revenue by recommending the right product to new prospects. Recommendation engine will help marketers have a higher ROI. The likelihood of a customer to purchase a product depends on when, where, and how the product was introduced. Barilliance found that 31% of revenues of online retailers have been produced from personalized product recommendations. Based on a report by McKinsey, Amazon recommendation engine has created 35% of its revenue (Salesforce: Solutions).

It is important to know which type of recommendations is better to use and where. Barilliance studies have found that recommendations with the title "what customers ultimately buy" had the highest engagement results. When there is no information on the website visitor or the new subscriber, use the "best seller" category recommendations. It is recommended to use personalized recommendation in email communication to subscribers (Serrano, 2018). One place that recommendations can be used easily is when sending a shipping confirmation email to a customer. A portion of this email can be used for showing products that are recommended based on the customer's shopping history and the products that are included in the shipping.

Lead Capture

Using the data of existing customers that have the highest values, AI can help sales team to find the potential new prospects that match a similar pattern of the highest scored consumers. Almost all CRM providers will have attributes and properties that will help identifying the value of each customer (Columbus, 2018). Third-party data is helpful to find a new demographic for your market, having access to data of consumers that are interested in similar products will give marketers ability to expand the reach and find potential new demographics (Lotame, 2018).

Forecasting

First-party data lets the marketer predict the future behavior of an audience. Using this can show that person A hasn't been engaged with your product, marketer can think of a method to reengage them using the consumer data collected for this person. Another example, imagine a customer browsing the website for a specific product and has placed it in the shopping cart. However, the product was not checked out for few days. In this regard, a communication can be sent to the customer reminding them that this product is in their cart: if the person still doesn't act on the abandoned cart, perhaps the marketer should offer an incentive (i.e., price reduction, free shipping).

Finding the pattern in the data using AI can help marketer personalize the content for better engagement (Lotame, 2018). By mixing the historical data on sales and price, and the use of machine learning algorithm, the sales can be forecasted more accurately. This will help companies to invest more into new products or products that show a better outcome in the forecast (Columbus, 2018).

Scoring

AI can use first-party data to predict the future behavior of the prospect. Salesforce marketing cloud is using the data in several different places to help you keep the customers loyal and eager to engage. Using interaction studio, the entire journey of a customer can be personalized based on the actions taken. By using engagement scoring, marketers can predict who are their highest ranking customers in the engagement and who are the ones that they might lose. Having this information will help marketers to try to re-engage with the high-risk customers by offering incentives to them (Salesforce: Products).

Pricing

Using data available, sales and marketing can optimize the price better using AI and machine learning algorithm. AI can use the purchase history, promotions, coupons, and pricing data to offer a more adaptable price to a prospect (Columbus, 2018).

Risks

Known vs. Unknown

Consumers' behaviors offline and online are attached to a known and unknown users and that makes it harder to make use of all the data available to marketers. One way to mitigate this issue is the use of Third party data as discussed earlier in this chapter. As you navigate a website, if there is a tracking code on the website, your online presence is being gathered and stored in a database, like the IGoDigital servers. If this person at some point during the time of being online signs up or logs in to his/her account, that last behavior data will be connected. When a user browse a website, there will be a cookie associated with the user, and there is a risk on inconsistency specially when the person clears the cookie or uses the incognito browser.

Lack of Historical Data

There might not have been anything in place for gathering information for marketing. This will make it difficult to use concepts like prediction and recommendations but it is never too late to start the process, so data can be collected.

Third-Party vs. First-Party Data

The amount of data available to marketers for first party is limited so to capture more customers, marketers rely on third-party data that comes with its risks. As discussed earlier, GDPR will have a direct impact on third-party data that will make it harder or even impossible to use this data. First-party data is more secure from GDPR law since it is the data that was collected by this company.

References

Accenture. "Making It Personal," Accenture: Pulse Check 2018. 2018. www.accenture. com/t20161011T222718__w__/us-en/_acnmedia/PDF-34/Accenture-Pulse-Check-Dive-Key-Findings-Personalized-Experiences.pdf.

Alaimo, Dan. "Chatbots to Talk up $11B in Cost Savings by 2023," Retail Dive. 2018. www.retaildive.com/news/chatbots-to-talk-up-11b-in-cost-savings-by-2023/527125/.

Bendici, Ray. "Rise of the Machines," UB Technology. pp. 53–55. 2018. www. universitybusiness.com.

Benes, Ross. "Why Building AI Products Requires Big Investment: Application is Making Inroads in Marketing Technology," eMarketer. 2018.

Biselli, Luca, Nicola Dragoni, Pier Paolo Greco, Antonio Marraffa, Manuel Mazzara, and Nafees Qamar. "Social Networks and Collective Intelligence: A Return to the Agora," Newcastle University: Technical Report Series. 2012.

Brown, Eileen. "Survey Shows that Three-Quarters of Businesses Improve Revenue with AI," ZDNet. 2018. www.zdnet.com/article/survey-shows-that-three-quarters-of-businesses-improve-revenue-with-ai/.

Columbus, Louis, "10 Ways Machine Learning Is Revolutionizing Sales", Forbes. 2018. www.forbes.com/sites/louiscolumbus/2018/12/26/10-ways-machine-learning-is-revolutionizing-sales.

Hinchey, Michael G., Roy Sterritt and Chris Rouff. "Swarms and Swarm Intelligence," *Computer*, vol. 40, no. 4, pp. 111–113. 2007.

Infosys. "Rethinking Retail: Insights from Customers and Retailers Into an Omni-Channel Shopping Experience," Infosys. 2013. www.infosys.com/newsroom/press-releases/Documents/genome-research-report.pdf.

Kose, Utku and Selcuk Sert. "Intelligent Content Marketing with Artificial Intelligence," Scientific Cooperation for the Future in the Social Sciences. 2016.

Lenskold Group. "2012 Lead Generation Marketing Effectiveness Study," Lenskold Group. 2012. http://revmarketer.pedowitzgroup.com/rs/pedowitzgroup2/images/LenskoldGroup_Lead_Gen_Effectiveness_Report_2012.pdf.

Lotame. "1st Party Data, 2nd Party Data, 3rd Party Data: What Does It All Mean?" Lotame. 2018. www.lotame.com/1st-party-2nd-party-3rd-party-data-what-does-it-all-mean/.

Miller, Jaden, "What Are Lookalike Audiences, and When Should You Use Them?", 9Clouds. 2018. https://9clouds.com/blog/what-are-lookalike-audiences-when-should-you-use-them/.

Plessis, Charmaine du. "The Role of Content Marketing in Social Media Content Communities," *South African Journal of Information Movement*, vol. 19, no. 1, pp. 1–17. 2017.

Preimesberger, Chris. "State of Chatbots in 2018: Rapidly Moving into the Mainstream." EWeek, p. 1. 2018.

"Product Recommendation Engines to Improve Customer Relationships," Salesforce: Solutions.

Redman, Thomas C. "Bad Data Costs the U.S. $3 Trillion Per Year," *Harvard Business Review*. 2016. https://hbr.org/2016/09/bad-data-costs-the-u-s-3-trillion-per-year.

Ross, Casey. "IBM Pitched its Watson Supercomputer as a Revolution in Cancer Care. It's Nowhere Close," STAT. 2017. www.statnews.com/2017/09/05/watson-ibm-cancer/.

Salesforce: Products, "Meet Interaction Studio," www.salesforce.com/products/marketing-cloud/customer-interaction/.

Satu, M. S., M. H. Parvez and Shamim Al-Mamun, "Review of Integrated Applications with AIML Based Chatbot," *2015 International Conference on Computer and Information Engineering (ICCIE)*, Rajshahi, pp. 87–90. 2015.

Schachinger, Kristine. "A Complete Guide to the Google RankBrain Algorithm," *Search Engine Journal*. 2017, www.searchenginejournal.com/google-algorithm-history/rank brain/#close.

Segall, Richard S., Qingyu Zhang, "Web Mining Technologies for Customer and Marketing Surveys," *Kybernetes*, vol. 38, no. 6, pp. 925–949. 2009.

Serrano, Stephan, "Personalized Product Recommendation Tips and Stats" Barilliance. 2018 www.barilliance.com/personalized-product-recommendations-stats/.

Spyridaki, Kalliopi. "GDPR and AI: Friends, Foes or Something in Between?" SAS Insights. www.sas.com/en_us/insights/articles/data-management/gdpr-and-ai--friends--foes-or-something-in-between-.html.

Statista. "Digital Channels in Which Personalized Communication is Used Worldwide as of March 2018," *Statista*. 2019. www.statista.com/statistics/451788/digital-marketing-channelswith-personalized-communication/.

Sullivan, Laurie, "SEO Improvements Link to AI; Strategies Still Too Complicated", MediaPost. Apr. 2017, www.mediapost.com/publications/article/298366/seo-improvements-link-to-ai-strategies-still-too.html.

Weizenbaum, Joseph. "ELIZA--A Computer Program For the Study of Natural Language Communication Between Man and Machine," *Commungicatins of the ACM*, Vol. 9, no. 1, pp. 525–526. 1966.

WorkMarket. "WorkMarket's 2020 In(Sight) Report: What AI & Automation Really Mean for Work," WorkMarket. 2017. www.forbes.com/sites/waldleventhal/2017/08/03/how-automation-could-save-your-business-4-million-annually/#40dadadb3807.

Yuniarthe, Yodhi, "Application of Artificial Intelligence (AI) in Search Engine Optimization (SEO)," *2017 International Conference on Soft Computing*, Intelligent System and Information Technology (ICSIIT), Denpasar, pp. 96–101. 2017.

Chapter 8

Artificial Intelligence in Healthcare

Rashida Peete, Kasia Majowski,
Laura Lauer, and Annie Jay
Impact Advisors

Contents

Introduction

As we have learned, artificial intelligence (AI) is on its way to become the leading method for handling various tasks as society continually strives to advance technologically – operating with more automation. Through its abundant capacity, artificial intelligence, or AI as it is more commonly known, will affect each sector from opposing angles as it develops its groundings. In this chapter, we will discuss how this continuously growing phenomenon will penetrate the complex industry of healthcare. We will examine the use of AI in healthcare from the perspective of the following pillars: Policies and Security, Patient Care, and AI's overall longevity in this challenging domain. Within each section, information will be provided to clarify aspects that must be considered or act as a "priority" regarding changes or additions in processes or interactions inside the healthcare system.

Policies and Security

Health Insurance Portability and Affordability Act (HIPAA)

In thinking about healthcare, one of the most critical acting components is HIPAA or the Health Insurance Portability and Affordability Act. Enacted in August 1996, this act was created to ensure the privacy of patient information among other integrity-imposed items regarding patient care. The act is subdivided into five sections:

I. Health Care Access, Portability, and Renewability
II. Preventing Health Care Fraud and Abuse, Administrative Simplification, Medical Liability Reform
III. Tax-Related Health Provisions
IV. Application and Enforcement of Group Health Plan Requirements
V. Revenue Offsets

This act speaks to the depth of complexity that surrounds healthcare (Rouse, 2017). Since information is a vital portion of healthcare, it is equally important that ample security is supplied to protect sensitive information that is hosted in the form of medical records, corresponding files, and forms pertaining to medical care. This is essentially why HIPAA was put in place – it supplies a "protective net". It should be noted that this security measure is separated by standards that companies and institutions should abide by in addition to privacy standards for individuals. On the business spectrum, this is known as HIPAA compliance, which supplies specified rules and regulations that any entity handling *protected health information (PHI)* must *secure*. For individuals, such standards are known as the *security rule* which ensures the medical privacy and protection that we are all familiar with when it comes to healthcare (Groot, 2018).

Keeping all of this in mind, it can be said that AI begs the concern of whether implementing AI into an already rigorous and complex environment will be able to uphold the current security measures and protection? Or will it make the health-care industry more susceptible to vulnerabilities that exist with technology? And finally, how compatible will AI be with healthcare compliance and policies in general? To answer these questions, the general premise for the goal of AI is to enhance processes for any capacity it has been executed. For example, *MYCIN*, one of the first AI subsets to be created, did just that. The goal for this product was to recognize bacteria that may lead to numerous infectious diseases (Teich, 2018). Although it was a success and exceeded expectations, the difficulty laid in the ability to parse regulatory standards and additional healthcare policies.

As mentioned above, HIPAA compliance and industry policies are the *beating core* of the healthcare industry. Thus, for AI to be fruitful, and dare we say a "tremendous benefit", it would be remiss for it to negate such standards. Due to this breadth of concerns, developers and connoisseurs of AI work diligently to mitigate these issues. However, as an article published by Stanford University Law School points out, "The threat spectrum is deep and wide...The burden here is far from trivial as the covered entity and its business associates are directed to analyze the 'probability and criticality of potential risks'" (Kahana, 2016).

Technology and the expansion of technology will continue to pose new risks and threats just as much as sensitive information will forever be a targeted entity for lurking predators. There is a fear, by all means justifiable, that AI may not be thoroughly adequate or feasible to withstand the demands that exist. However, this is a chance that many deem "worth-a-shot" if it eases the burden in healthcare. The potential that exists in AI for the betterment of healthcare is said to supersede such hesitancies. Research shows that introducing an AI element to healthcare can provide the added benefit of:

I. Predicting future aliments through analysis of current health status to provide preventative care or measures
II. Publishing research of causes, symptoms, and effects of life-threatening diseases such as cancer
III. Producing medical solutions such as EMR (electronic medical records), just to list a few (Joshi, 2018).

Moreover, the idea of growth is to develop precautions and adjust our standards to guard against instances or concerns. However, the hassle with applying this theory to healthcare and technology as a united front is that no one person, or many for that matter, is able to predict issues that may arise. Overall, will AI introduce new complications and risk to healthcare institutions and facilities? This is quite possible. However, these same institutions and governances have resources available to develop and modify regulations that account for such changes. Although this may be a daunting and difficult task, it is not impossible.

Patient Protection and Affordable Care Act (PPACA)

The Patient Protection and Affordable Care Act (PPACA), or more commonly known as the Affordable Care Act (ACA), was signed into law by President Barack Obama on March 23, 2010. This law worked to reform the U.S. healthcare system. From a health insurance reform perspective, the PPACA law sought to cover uninsured U.S. citizens and provide a greater pool of benefit options; all while lowering overall healthcare costs. The health system portion of the act focuses on improving quality and efficiency standards within healthcare facilities, paying greater attention to public health and preventative care initiatives.

AI may be the answer to further improve coverage options and overall healthcare facility and treatment quality while maintaining low costs. According to The Medical Futurist, "with an unprecedented amount of data available, combined with advances in natural language processing and social awareness algorithms, applications of AI will become increasingly more useful to consumers" (2016). These applications will likely come in the form of big data utilization for the improvement of quality and patient experience. For example, as we continue to cultivate large amounts of big data, data scientists are able to better assist the goals of the PPACA. One such application of big data utilization can be seen through the mining of patient medical records. This type of mining would enable facilities to better streamline processes such as patient intake, medicine tracking, and distribution. AI could also be utilized to improve overall efficiency by replacing or counteracting repetitive jobs (Artificial Intelligence Will Redesign Healthcare, 2018). What may take an administrative assistant 15 min, such as electronic medical record input, could take AI seconds.

While AI has many promising applications in the healthcare field, patient privacy and security is still a main concern. If the data that is collected during mining processes gets into the wrong hands, many patient health records could be at risk. If AI is to be integrated into major components of the healthcare system, the security of a patient's private information should be the center of all policy and process creation.

Occupational Safety and Health Administration (OSHA)

The Occupational Safety and Health Act of 1970 was an initiative by Congress to create safe and hazard-free workplaces for all U.S. workers (About OSHA, n.d.). This was prompted by public pressure on Congress due to increased death and injury worker cases. Through this initiative by Congress and the general public, the Occupational Safety and Health Administration, also known as OSHA, was founded on April 28, 1971, to establish and administer standards of health and safety throughout U.S.-based workplaces.

In many industries, AI is being integrated into OSHA policies, procedures, and compliance standards (Weldler, 2018). Microsoft is working with the OSHA compliance board to adapt AI into many aspects of the industry to improve safety and health standards (Meyerstein, 2017). At the 2017 Microsoft developer conference, Andrea Carl, Microsoft's Director of Commercial Communications, showcased how cameras, networked devices such as phones and machines, can utilize AI. This AI-based software tracks employee and equipment activity to prevent accidents within the workplace, as well as gathers data to improve efficiency.

While projects, such as Microsoft's, can offer major improvements in safety and efficiency, privacy is still a concern. Should workers be susceptible to being tracked and analyzed while in the workplace? Will it decrease employee morale within the workplace? Who will own and store employee-based data? These are questions that must be asked as AI becomes more prevalent within multiple industries.

Compliance Officer

With the level of policy, governance, and personnel required for an organization to function and meet its business objectives accordingly, someone or a team of individuals must ensure that all precautions and corrective procedures are followed; especially in a *high stakes* culpability environment as healthcare. The title for the said individual(s) is compliance officer. This is the person who maintains the integrity of policies and regulations within a company or organization. Duties that fall under their responsibility may include, but are not limited to, maintaining clear communication of company principles, conducting internal/external audits, and involving disclaimers when necessary (Chen, 2018). In the realm of healthcare, these elected officials ensure that medical institutions and all associated partners are well aware of the standards required to protect patients and the ethical practices are followed. The emergence of this role was derived from the responsibility of HIPAA. Legislators of HIPAA wanted to ensure that this act is followed in its entirety alongside other working environment regulating acts including OSHA and Health Information Technology for Economic and Clinical Health (HITECH) (American Academy of Professional Coders, 2018).

In short, a compliance officer is a governing body that maintains industry integrity by following safeguards and protective laws. As we continue to elude the revolving theme of privacy and protection regarding healthcare, the looming question, then, is what makes a compliance officer beneficial to patient care? Or more so, what role do they play regarding patients? To answer this question, a compliance officer is pertinent to patient care and medical establishments due to their level of responsibility to patient privilege and confidentiality. As we've stated earlier, their sole purpose is to make certain that organizations adhere to their regulatory framework – for the case of healthcare, this happens to be *confidentiality*. Not just confidentiality regarding communication between doctors and other medical professionals, but translating information to providers as well. As patient information is processed from *point A* through *point Z*, the compliance officer conducts audits necessary to enforce industry regulation.

Tying this understanding to the possible interaction for integrating AI to healthcare – like the HIPAA law – most concerns point back to security provisions. Mainly, whether AI will be compatible with already-enforced security measures or will it introduce an added layer of complexity by extending vulnerabilities? Unfortunately, there is no definite answer. The possibility for fault will remain undefinable due to the nature of technology and the stringencies and complexity of healthcare. Although the previous statement is undeniable, it should not be taken as a reason to refrain from the idea of AI in healthcare. The medical industry continuously remains underdeveloped on the technology plane. In fact, updating to more modern systems to "catch up" to the ever-evolving technology stream often requires more time and resources resulting in prolonged downtime for medical processing and care than if the industry remains current with the growth of technology – or at least more abreast than they are presently. All in all, the effects of AI on compliance can be seen as a packaged deal complete with:

I. Major policy adjustments to accommodate the new technology.
II. Devising a framework that compliments current regulatory provisions but supports AI procedures.
III. Leveraging complexity and protection of sensitive health information.

While making sure that the premise of AI, to ease processing procedures and enhance research and knowledge, AI must remain intact without introducing considerable liabilities.

Applications of AI in Healthcare

Physical Artificial Intelligence

Generally speaking, AI in healthcare stems from two main categories, physical and virtual AI (Hamet & Tremblay, 2017). Physical AI is mostly made up of robots, including robot assistance and nanorobots (Hamet & Tremblay, 2017). Some robots currently used in a healthcare environment include robots for destroying germs, therapy, transportation, and surgery. Xenex has created a line of robots that use UV rays to kill bacteria and reduce healthcare-associated infections (HIAs). The robot is used to combat infections from areas including methicillin-resistant *Staphylococcus aureus* (MRSA), *Clostridium difficile* infection (CDI), and surgical site infections (SSIs) (Xenex, 2019). PARO is a robot used to mimic the healing effects of animal therapy in environments where introducing live animals is not ideal. PARO looks and sounds like a baby harp seal and uses sensors to interact with people and their environment. Some benefits of the robot include reducing patient stress, improving relaxation, and socialization (PARO Robots U.S., Inc., 2014). In a healthcare environment, there is a need to transport clinical supplies, meals, and other materials around the facility every day.

A mobile robot designed by Aethon, named TUG, is currently used to securely deliver a variety of items including linens, medications, and specimens within healthcare facilities (Aethon Inc., 2018).

Let's take a closer look at a robot used by surgeons in operating rooms around the world, the *da Vinci* Surgical System. We will start with the basic functions. At the start of surgery, the system provides vision magnification for the surgeon shown in 3D and uses tiny incisions to work in the patient. Then, the surgeon can maneuver using small robotic instruments. One cited benefit is that these instruments have more range of motion and precise movement than a human hand. The types of surgery that can be completed using *da Vinci* surgery include cardiac, colorectal, general, gynecologic, head and neck, thoracic, and urologic (Intuitive Surgical, Inc., 2019). Debates have been raised whether minimally invasive surgery with or without robot assistance makes a significant difference in patient outcomes or the bottom line. There is little evidence to make a clear distinction of whether minimally invasive surgery is better for patients with traditional methods or a robot. Unfortunately, surgery with a robot can increase costs by an estimated $3,000–$6,000 more. This questions whether the performance of a *da Vinci* robot provides enough value to offset the increased cost to patients and hospitals (Scott, 2016).

Now that we have examined larger physical robots in AI, it is time to think small…extremely small. The use of nanotechnology has been increasing in the medical field. The National Nanotechnology Initiative (NNI) is an initiative through the U.S. government that defines the size of nanotechnology to be 1–100 nm (Saadeh & Vyas, 2014). The International System of Units defines a nanometer as one-billionth of a meter. To put the size into perspective, NNI gives examples that "a strand of human DNA is 2.5 nanometers in diameter" and "a human hair is approximately 80,000–100,000 nanometers wide" (United States National Nanotechnology Initiative, 2019). A nanorobot used in healthcare requires being "sized" on a nanoscale. The nanorobot also needs a control mechanism, so it can be directed on or within the human body to function in the way it was intended. This technology opens a range of applications within the medical field across different disciplines (Saadeh & Vyas, 2014).

Nanorobots have already been created that can be maneuvered with precision to transport cells throughout the body of laboratory mice. This affords healthcare the opportunity to be personalized in a way that has not been previously available. There are still more trials and testing to be done, but this can significantly affect the applications in healthcare over the next 5–10 years (Markman, 2018).

Virtual Artificial Intelligence

Virtual AI encompasses informatics, deep learning, directing health management systems, and assisting physicians with diagnosis and treatment plans (Hamet & Tremblay, 2017). Many countries use electronic health records (EHR), and some countries require EHR to be used by health providers. An EHR is a patient's information stored in a digital format including health history, treatments, medications, test results, images, and more. EHRs not only store valuable patient information but also include a variety of formats, and can accumulate a large amount of data over time. EHR can be used to make effective healthcare decisions, but entering, accessing, and effectively evaluating all information in an EHR during the time given in one patient visit can be difficult for clinicians (Bhavaraju, 2018). Some healthcare organizations are investing in AI to evaluate the immense amounts of health information. By introducing AI, the hope is to aid in health decision and reduce the number of medical errors (Towers-Clark, 2018).

Virtual AI devices fall into two major categories: machine learning (ML) and natural language processing (NLP). Health information can be comprised of structured data or information that is presented in a set format. Some examples of structured health data include demographics, images, and genetic data. ML is used to assess data to make clinical decisions. Health information can also include unstructured data which does not have pre-determined content. Some examples of unstructured data in healthcare include clinical notes or medical journals. NLP is used to evaluate unstructured data and translate it into structured data; then, the information is evaluated using ML (Dong et al., 2017).

An example of applying ML and NLP is a study conducted predicting patient mortality rates in a surgical intensive care unit (SICU). Comparing health information for patients that lived and patients that died, variables were identified, weighted, and used in algorithms by ML to be significant predictors of mortality. NLP was used to assess clinical notes. The words "dilated" and "hemorrhage" were shown to be indicators of patient mortality (Parreco et al., 2018). ML can also be used for direct interaction with patients. Virtual nursing assistants are being used to personalize patient care. iCare Navigator is a platform that interacts with patients using a virtual image. The system applies ML to evaluate a patient's EHR to engage the person, determine the best time to educate them on a health condition, and how to manage their care (Kiger, 2018).

Disease Assessment

AI is used in numerous areas to study various diseases in healthcare. However, there are three disease areas that have produced the most research including cancer, neurology, and cardiology. All three areas are prominent causes of death. Detecting and diagnosing these diseases quickly can have a major impact on the patient's survival (Dong et al., 2017). According to the World Stroke Organization, an estimated one in six people will have a stroke in their lifetime and someone dies from a stroke every 6 s. The World Stroke Organization also states that "stroke is one of the leading causes of long-term disability worldwide" (*Facts and figures about stroke*, 2012). Time is critical for the detection of a stroke and can mean the difference between a patient recovering, being disabled long-term, or dying. A product called Viz LVO is using AI software to view images, like CT scans, and automatically detect large vessel occlusion (LVO) strokes. Viz LVO also notifies hospital specialists and connects the patient's physician. The use of this process has decreased the patient's diagnosis and treatment response time by hours (Walter, 2018).

Physical and virtual AI has a wide range of applications in the healthcare industry. AI is already being utilized and making a difference in healthcare. There are plenty of problems to solve; Is AI actually the solution? Have we reached the point where we can place a person's life in the (virtual) hands of AI?

AI Considerations for Healthcare Longevity

Is AI Here to Stay in Healthcare?

The term Artificial Intelligence was first coined in 1956 by a group of mathematicians during the Dartmouth Summer Research Project (Knapp, 2006). Since that summer, AI has seen many cycles, but this cycle may be more than hype for healthcare (Derrington, 2017).

A paper that was supported by the U.S. Department of Health and Human Services stated that a few reasons that AI might be here to stay in the healthcare environment are:

- The frustration with current or legacy medical systems and their associated workflows;
- The ubiquity of networked devices; and
- The acceptance of – and eagerness for – technology in our lives (Derrington, 2017).

These reasons are certainly compelling to look toward the future in the healthcare industry, which has been notoriously slow in progress.

Medical technology systems are built to replicate the paper-based workflows that came before them. However, unlike the paper-based workflows, these medical technology systems can take in and store a vast amount of data. AI can use the data generated by the traditional medical systems, such as when clinician's screen patients and assigns a diagnosis and treatment to that patient (Dong et al., 2017).

It is currently the clinician's responsibility to interpret the massive amount of patient data that is stored in any particular system, which is time-consuming. This is where AI can enter into the workflow because it is built on algorithms that can review and analyze a vast amount of data (Dong et al., 2017). These computer algorithms can review data far more quickly than a human ever could. This means that the AI system can find patterns and help clinicians diagnose patients more quickly than they could without the assistance of AI (Dong et al., 2017). By using the data that is collected by the legacy medical systems and workflows, AI can quickly produce an analysis that doctors can use to inform their diagnoses to patients.

Fed by data-rich systems, AI would be able to flourish in the healthcare industry because of the sheer amount of data that is produced. Hospitals (and their parent health systems) house any number of networked devices, which – most of the time – allow for the sharing of data between medical systems (Derrington, 2017). This data sharing can create large data sets, which AI systems can use to analyze and predict outcomes and patterns. The more data that an AI system can analyze and "learn", the more accurate it becomes.

The number of networked devices and the amount of data that is stored in medical systems have led to more data sharing between entities (Derrington, 2017). Some examples of this include population health initiatives, such as Health Information Exchanges, or specific groups within hospital systems set up to collect patient data from across their own network (Bresnick, 2019). These trends have encouraged data sharing. Most health systems have a team of interface analysts hired specifically to ensure that all systems are sharing and communicating data, at least in one standardized direction (Derrington, 2017).

Hospital systems will continue to merge and standardize. Government mandates will continue to push health systems to total digitalization of patient data. Society has a willingness, and perhaps even eagerness, to share our information. All of these factors encourage the use of AI data-driven systems.

Challenges to AI in Healthcare

With the constant collection of patient data and the rise in population health initiatives, AI use in healthcare seems inevitable. It is faced with some challenges, especially around data quality, standardization, and security.

The major challenge from a technical point of view stems from the amount of data that is produced and stored surrounding healthcare – beginning with the amount of usable training data that is required to "teach" an AI system. AI systems require large data sets to achieve high-quality results (Derrington, 2017, Wahl et al., 2018). Although all medical systems produce or collect some kind of data, it is often not standardized enough for AI systems. Unstandardized data may be a result of varied sources (i.e., EMR data where multiple hospital departments may enter data on one patient).

Per Dutt (2018), usable, "clean", data needs to have the following qualities, especially in healthcare:

- Accuracy – data must be recorded accurately to get accurate results.
- Completeness – data must be recorded completely to get complete results.
- Consistency – over time, the data must be recorded in a standardized way.
- Timeliness – if the data changes, the AI system will need to adapt to read the new data format.

These qualifications usually make AI impractical to use for many hospital systems on a day-to-day basis in today's environment (Derrington, 2017). In most settings, clinicians are not typically focused on the cleanliness of the data they collect, but on how they interpret and react to the data they collect.

Data quality and standardization is only one of the challenges that AI faces in healthcare. Another significant challenge that AI faces is the rigorous approval and validation process that accompanies the use of patient data (Derrington, 2017). Patient data is necessary to analyze trends, but health systems must consider data security, user access restrictions, and code compliance (Dutt, 2018). All of these considerations take time and resources to design, build, and implement into a new process. Many hospitals and health systems do not have the time or inclination to collect data and implement the processes to enable an AI system.

Although AI faces many challenges in the healthcare environment, there is some AI progress in the healthcare field, especially at larger, more research-based institutions. For example, the Cleveland Clinic implemented a Center for Artificial Intelligence. This center is focused on applying AI to the healthcare environment (Bresnick, 2019). As larger institutions continue to implement AI, they set precedents and guidelines for smaller health systems and hospitals to follow and implement, making AI a more attainable goal and improving patient care.

References

About OSHA. (n.d.). Retrieved December 18, 2018, from www.osha.gov/about.html.

Aethon Inc. (2018). TUG. Retrieved January 2019, from aethon.com: https://aethon.com/mobile-robots-for-healthcare/.

American Academy of Professional Coders. (2018). Healthcare Compliance. Retrieved from AAPC - Advancing the Business of Healthcare: www.aapc.com/healthcare-compliance/healthcare-compliance.aspx.

Artificial Intelligence Will Redesign Healthcare. (2018, July 26). Retrieved December 18, 2018, from https://medicalfuturist.com/artificial-intelligence-will-redesign-healthcare.

Bhavaraju, S. R. (2018, September 18). From subconscious to conscious to artificial intelligence: a focus on electronic health records. *Neurology India*. doi:10.4103/0028-3886.241377.

Bresnick, J. (2019, March 13). Cleveland Clinic Creates Artificial Intelligence Innovation Center. Retrieved from Health IT Analytics: https://healthitanalytics.com/news/cleveland-clinic-creates-artificial-intelligence-innovation-center.

Chen, J. (2018, July 20). Compliance Officer. Retrieved from Investopedia: www.investopedia.com/terms/c/compliance-officer.asp.

Derrington, D. (2017, December). *Artificial Intelligence for Health and Health Care* [PDF]. Retrieved from www.healthit.gov/sites/default/files/jsr-17-task-002_aiforhealthandhealthcare12122017.pdf.

Dong, Q., Dong, Y., Jiang, F., Jiang, Y., Li, H., Ma, S., Shen, H., Wang, Y., Wang, Y., & Zhi, H. (2017, June 21). Artificial intelligence in healthcare: past, present and future. *Stroke and Vascular Neurology, 2*. doi:10.1136/svn-2017-000101.

Dutt, R. (2018, January 8). *AI: The Challenge of Data*. Retrieved from: www.infoworld.com/article/3246706/artificial-intelligence/ai-the-challenge-of-data.html.

Groot, J. D. (2018, September 25). What is HIPAA Compliance? Retrieved from Digital Guardian: https://digitalguardian.com/blog/what-hipaa-compliance.

Hamet, P., & Tremblay, J. (2017). Artificial Intelligence in Medicine. *Metabolism: Clinical and Experimental, 69, 36–40*. doi:10.1016/j.metabol.2017.01.011.

Intuitive Surgical, Inc. (2019, January 31). *da Vinci Surgery: Minimally Invasive Surgery.* Retrieved from da Vinci Surgery: www.davincisurgery.com.

Joshi, N. (2018, August 15). *The Challenges of Artifical Intelligence To Succeed in Healthcare.* Retrieved from BBN Times: www.bbntimes.com/en/technology/the-challenges-of-artificial-intelligence-to-succeed-in-healthcare.

Kahana, E. (2016, March 20). *HIPAA & Deep Neural AI.* Retrieved from Stanford Law School: https://law.stanford.edu/2016/03/20/hipaa-deep-neural-ai/.

Kiger, P. (2018, May 21). *Animated Avatars Guide Hospital Patients' Recoveries.* Retrieved from AARP: www.aarp.org/health/conditions-treatments/info-2018/hospital-artificial-intelligence-telehealth.html.

Knapp, S. (2006, July 24). Artificial Intelligence: Past, Present, and Future. *Vox of Dartmouth The Newspaper for Faculty and Staff, July 24 Issue.* Retrieved from www.dartmouth.edu/~vox/0607/0724/ai50.html.

Marksman, J. (2018, July 31). Killer Nanorobots are Coming for your Cancer. *Forbes.*

Meyerstein, A. (2017, June 08). *Microsoft AI Getting into Workplace Safety?* Retrieved December 18, 2018, from www.safetylawmatters.com/2017/06/microsoft-ai-getting-workplace-safety/.

PARO Robots U.S., Inc. (2014). *PARO Therapeutic Robot.* Retrieved February 2, 2019, from parorobots.com: www.parorobots.com/index.asp.

Parreco, J., Hidalgo, A., Kozol, R., Namias, N., & Rattan, R. (2018, July). Predicting mortality in the surgical intensive care unit using artificial intelligence and natural language processing of physician documentation. *American Surgeon, 84, 1190–1194.*

Rouse, M. (2017, July). *HIPAA: Health Insurance Portability and Accountability Act.* Retrieved from Tech Target: https://searchhealthit.techtarget.com/definition/HIPAA.

Saadeh, Y., & Vyas, D. (2014, September 8). *Nanorobotic Applications in Medicine: Current Proposals and Designs.* doi:10.1166/ajrs.2014.1010.

Scott, C. (2016, August 10). *Is da Vinci Robotic Surgery a Revolution or a Rip-Off?* Retrieved from healthline: www.healthline.com/health-news/is-da-vinci-robotic-surgery-revolution-or-ripoff-021215#1.

Teich, D. A. (2018, March 20). *Artificial Intelligence (AI), Healthcare and Regulatory Compliance.* Retrieved from Forbes: www.forbes.com/sites/tiriasresearch/2018/03/20/artificial-intelligence-ai-healthcare-and-regulatory-compliance/#3fb892004f66.

Towers-Clark, C. (2018, November 22). Using Artificial Intelligence to Fix Healthcare. *Forbes.*

United States National Nanotechnology Initiative. (2019). *Size of the Nanoscale.* Retrieved from www.nano.gov: www.nano.gov/nanotech-101/what/nano-size.

Wahl, B., Cossy-Gantner, A., Germann, S., & Schwalbe, N. R. (2018, August 29). Artificial intelligence (AI) and global health: how can AI contribute to health in resource-poor settings? *BMJ Global Health, 3(4), e000798.* doi:10.1136/bmjgh-2018-000798.

Walter, M. (2018, November 20). *Viz.ai Artificial Intelligence Stroke Software Helping Doctors Win Race Against Time.* Retrieved from Radiology Business: www.radiologybusiness.com/sponsored/22221/topics/artificial-intelligence/vizai-artificial-intelligence-stroke-software.

Weldler, T. (2018, October 09). *Artificial Intelligence in Workers' Compensation and OSHA Compliance*. Retrieved December 18, 2018, from https://modwatchsystems.com/ artificial-intelligence-in-workers-compensation-and-osha-compliance/.

World Stroke Organization. (2012). *Facts and Figures about Stroke*. Retrieved from World Stroke Organization: www.world-stroke.org/component/content/article/16-forpatients/84-facts-and-figures-about-stroke.

Xenex. (2019, January 30). Xenex Disinfection Systems. Retrieved from www.xenex.com: www.xenex.com/.

Chapter 9

Artificial Intelligence and Medical Devices

Dushyanth Maratt
ITC Infotech

Contents

The medical devices industry is complex, regulated and one that has a direct impact on our health. The manufacturers of these medical devices aim to improve healthcare and the quality of life for human beings and animals. The first-known medical device dates to 1816 which was a stethoscope invented by a French doctor.[1] In today's world, the wearables are the new standard for medical devices. In this chapter, we will look at the types of medical devices, trends, and examples and the impact of Artificial Intelligence (AI) use in medical devices in the industry.

Medical Devices: An Industry Overview

The global medical device market is expected to reach an estimated $409.5 billion by 2023, and it is forecast to grow at a compound annual growth rate (CAGR) of 4.5% from 2018 to 2023.[2] Medical devices manufacturers have two broad sub-industries. One sub-industry supplies healthcare equipment to hospitals and patients in outpatient care. The other sub-industry is focused on the creation of new and more technologically advanced medical equipment to improve the efficiency and accuracy of patient care. The definition of a medical device manufacturer is evolving as well. Wearables like the Fitbit brought in a fresh perspective to manage activity and health, and we have now a number of smart devices that monitor our vitals from blood sugar to heart rhythms.

There are 20 medical device manufacturers in the Fortune 1000 for 2018. Johnson & Johnson, Abbot Laboratories, Danaher, and Stryker are some of the larger companies in this industry. The figure below gives you a random sampling of the type of equipment this industry builds.

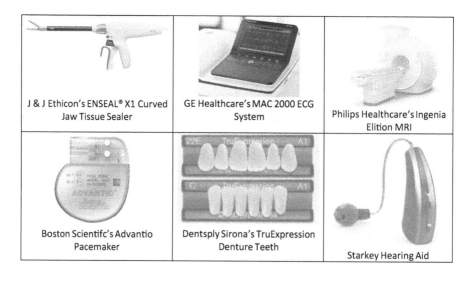

J & J Ethicon's ENSEAL® X1 Curved Jaw Tissue Sealer	GE Healthcare's MAC 2000 ECG System	Philips Healthcare's Ingenia Elition MRI
Boston Scientifc's Advantio Pacemaker	Dentsply Sirona's TruExpression Denture Teeth	Starkey Hearing Aid

The use of technology in the medical device industry has grown tremendously in the past 50 years. As in most industries, this growth surpasses advances made over the past 1,000 years. For example, microscopic devices have evolved from an optic microscope to an electron microscope which allows three-dimensional visualization of intracellular space. In the 1970s, medical technology started embracing computer technology. Medical devices are growing increasingly digitized with capabilities ranging from complex calculations, storing medical history, to performing robotic surgery with a high degree of precision.

Industry Outlook

The market size of the medical devices industry was \$156 billion in 2017,[3] and the outlook for the industry remains largely positive. A few key factors have contributed to this strong outlook and growth.

Factor 1: An Aging Population

The first key factor is the increase in the aging population globally. In the United States alone, the elderly population has grown significantly, while the "baby boomers" are moving into their 60s and 70s. The world's older population continues to grow at an unprecedented rate, and soon the largest population segment will be those considered elderly. The National Institute of Aging projects the number of people aged 65 or older to grow from an estimated 524 million in 2010 to nearly 1.5 billion in 2050, with most of the increase in developing countries.[4]

A large majority of our oldest population may lose their ability to live independently because of limited mobility, frailty, or other declines in physical or cognitive function. The increases in life expectancy and the sheer numeric growth of older populations in the demographic will likely raise the demand for care. Medical devices are foreseen to help provide care to this aging population. The demand for devices that can provide for outpatient care is increasing. Similarly, the elderly would increasingly use medical devices to help manage their health at home.

Factor 2: Increasing Regulation and Compliance

The medical devices industry is getting increasingly regulated. In the United States, the Food and Drug Administration's (FDA) Center for Devices and Radiological Health (CDHR) is responsible for protecting public health and assuring consumer confidence in devices marketed in the United States. The Patient Protection and Affordable Care Act had added a 2.3% excise tax on medical device manufacturers to pay for expanded healthcare insurance. The federal tax overhaul in late 2017 has not eliminated this tax either.

In Europe, comprehensive reform of the rules that govern the medical devices represents one of the most disruptive changes in recent times to the industry. The European Medical Device Regulation (EU MDR) replaced the current set of directives in February 2017, and companies will have 3 years to comply with a broad swathe of new rules for almost every kind of product in the medical device spectrum.

The costs associated with compliance may force some companies to take drastic steps, such as offloading product lines, avoiding markets, or even considering mergers or buyouts. The aftermath of the shake-up will be a stronger and more accountable medical devices industry. These companies have grasped that the increasing regulation represents not just a compliance challenge, but an opportunity to add value to the business at the same time.

Factor 3: Power Shift to Payers and Providers

For a long time, physician preferences were largely accepted, determined the treatment to administer and the equipment to purchase for providing care. Lately, that is no longer the case. Evidence-based care is edging out physician preferences as the decisive factor. Today, payers and providers are evaluating medical devices statistically on the basis of safety and procedural efficacy as well as on cost.

Patients across America are being covered by Accountable Care Organizations (ACOs), which bring together doctors, hospitals, and healthcare providers to offer better coordinated and lower cost care. Under this dynamic, provider executives mandate purchasing decisions across the value chain, or at least constrain choices based on cost and preferred supplier lists. While physician's preferences still matter, their freedom to choose is no longer granted.

The move toward value-based care is allowing payers and providers to provide improved quality of care and better patient outcomes. Though medical device companies are facing uphill challenges in adjusting to the new value-based payment models, it provides opportunities for the companies by working closely with payers and providers to provide a holistic approach for patient care.

Factor 4: Cost and Price Pressures

Medical device manufacturers are facing cost and price pressures from a number of areas. In developed countries, healthcare systems under financial pressure are responding by exploring every opportunity to increase efficiencies and reduce costs. As they look to save money, hospital executives nationwide are looking at medical device costs. Hospitals are using value analysis committees to evaluate medical devices. The committees assess the devices based on clinical outcomes and cost benefits to a large degree. A rapidly growing middle class in the developing economies are demanding more medical devices. However, these economies have a higher degree of price sensitivity. Hospitals are also hoping to make the devices they own last longer. Refurbishing is a growing area of interest, which could potentially lead to fewer purchases, straining demand.

Device manufacturers are having to find new ways to maintain their competitiveness. They are paying new attention to the detailed design of their product ranges hoping to eliminate excess cost wherever possible across the supply chain. Some device manufacturers are exploring risk-based contracts with hospitals. The premise being that manufacturers will be penalized if the device does not deliver the expected outcome. This would lead to a higher cost for the manufacturer in the short term but would lead to better quality and innovation in the long term, giving them an edge over the competition. The goal for the device manufacturers is to ultimately gain the flexibility to sell profitably across markets.

These factors lead the medical device manufacturers to rethink their business model from a traditional equipment selling model to one that would offer more value to care providers and patients.

The Evolution to Smart Medical Devices

Device manufacturers have historically focused on an aspect of a disease or illness, whether is it equipment to help diagnose conditions or for patient care at hospitals or homes. As the need for value-based care increases, there becomes a need to look at diagnosis and care management holistically. Medical device manufacturers are having to focus on providing services and developing new technologies that would address the care continuum. Providers faced with value-based care and outcome-based reimbursements are forcing similar mandates on medical device manufacturers.

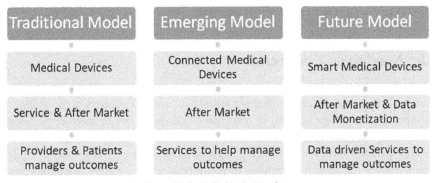

Evolving models for Medical Device Manufacturers

Traditionally, device manufacturers are in the business of generating revenue through selling equipment, aftermarket parts and servicing equipment. We are in the age where device manufacturers are having to evolve to (1) provide services to help manage outcomes and (2) build devices that are able to connect to the Internet and capture data based on their usage. A number of medical device companies are now providing services to help healthcare providers and patients to provide better outcomes. These services range from best practices in reducing infection risk management, standardizing on surgical procedures to supply chain optimization.

Connected Medical Devices and the Data Deluge

In the earlier sections, we looked at the factors affecting the medical devices industry. Given the various pressures of the industry, manufacturers are looking to eventually build "smart" medical devices. "Smart" devices can be defined as medical devices that have the ability to predict events, suggest actions to be taken to prevent untoward outcomes, or trigger actions based on happenings. "Smart" devices in effect would be medical devices that have intelligent (Artificial Intelligence) capabilities. The FDA defines AI as "A device or product that can imitate intelligent behavior or mimics human learning and reasoning. Artificial intelligence includes machine learning, neural networks, and natural language processing".[5] However, before devices can be made "smart", they have to be first "connected".

Connected devices are IoT (Internet of Things) enabled and have the ability to connect to the Internet and transmit data. Data transmitted by these devices could be data on how the patient is using the device or it could be about the function of the device itself. The emergence of 5G networks and LPWAN (low-power wide-area networks) is expected to accelerate the move to making medical devices connected. The challenges in making these devices connected would be around cyber security and securing patient data, regulatory approvals, and engineering the devices to integrate the connectivity hardware.

The Need to be Connected

Once these devices are "connected", they have the inherent capability to transmit data real time. The immediate benefit with the connected devices is the ability to monitor (1) the patient's health in real time or (2) the ability to monitor high-cost medical equipment. Monitoring patient health enables care providers to keep close tabs on patients and to react to health indicators more quickly. Monitoring equipment enables the service operations of equipment manufacturers to quickly react to equipment downtime and maintain uptime and availability of the high-cost equipment.

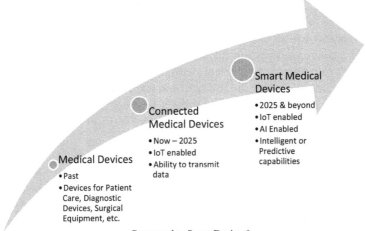

Connected to Smart Devices*

Years mentioned indicate when devices could possibly reach mainstream.

Over time, a significant amount of data would be collected from the connected devices. Applying AI (appropriate machine learning algorithms or other techniques) to this collected data opens up the possibilities to predict events. Some terms used to describe AI include computer-aided detection/diagnosis, statistical learning, deep learning, and smart algorithms.[6]

In the case of patient health, these AI-enabled devices could, for example, predict the possibility of a heart attack and help patients to take preventive measures thereby saving lives. High-cost medical equipment could have the capability to predict equipment failure or downtime and to proactively manage this. The ability to predict events and intelligently react to happenings provide the ultimate benefits to manufacturers and patients. Reaching this point is the goal which device manufactures are working by building connected and smart devices.

Evolving Regulation for Software in Medical Devices

In the United States, the FDA regulates the sale of medical devices and monitors the safety of all regulated medical products. Medical devices are categorized by the FDA into three classes – Class I, II, or III. They are classified based on their risks to patients and the regulatory controls required to provide adequate assurance of safety. Class I devices pose the lowest level of risk to the user, and Class III devices pose the highest risk. Examples[7] of devices across the three classes are:

- Class I: bandages, I.V. stand, sunglasses
- Class II: syringe, surgical mask, powered wheelchair
- Class III: heart valves, implantable neuromuscular stimulator

While AI-based medical devices hold tremendous potential, their regulation has challenged the FDA largely due to the fact that device amendments were crafted to address medical devices built a few decades back. These regulations were designed for hardware-based devices and frequent changes to technology design were infrequent. Today's landscape is different, with a significant number of products that are software based and have the ability to connect to and communicate with other devices or systems. These technology shifts have caused the FDA to re-evaluate its approach to regulating software. Listed below are regulations and guidance from the FDA in recent years on this subject.

- The 21st Century Cures Act ("Cures Act")[8] was enacted by the Congress in December 2016 and amended the Federal Food, Drug, and Cosmetic Act. This act contains provisions clarifying the FDA's jurisdiction over digital health products and excludes certain type of medical software from the definition of device.
- Draft guidance for Clinical and Patient Decision Support Software[9] aims to identify types of decision support software functionalities that (1) do not meet the definition of a device as amended by the Cures Act; (2) may meet the definition of a device, but the FDA does not intend to enforce compliance; and (3) devices that the FDA intends to focus its regulatory oversight on. AI-based devices may fall under this category if the software enables the user to independently review clinical recommendations provided among other things.
- The FDA's CDRH has outlined the Digital Health Innovation Action Plan[10] to outline the FDA's approach to ensure that patients, consumers and healthcare consumers have access to safe and high-quality digital health products. The FDA's focus on digital health is being driven by the fact that devices increasingly have connectivity features (i.e. the ability to connect and transmit data to other devices and systems) enabled.
- Guidance for Software as a Medical Device (SAMD)[11]: The use of SAMD is on the rise and is defined as "software intended to be used for one or more medical purposes that perform these purposes without being part of a hardware medical device". Given the unique features of SAMD that extend beyond a traditional medical device, regulators globally recognized the need to converge on a common framework to promote patient safety and innovation.
- Digital Health Software Precertification (Pre-Cert) Program[12]: Version 1. of the Software Precertification (Pre-Cert) Pilot Program explains how the FDA has re-imagined ways of regulating digital health products. This pilot program will help to develop a future regulatory model for efficient regulatory oversight of software-based medical devices. The FDA had selected nine companies to participate in the pilot program including Apple, Fitbit, Johnson & Johnson, and Roche.

AI Adoption across Categories of Medical Devices

We will now look at several examples of how the industry has started using AI. Medical imaging is perhaps one of the areas where AI has been put to use to detect several conditions. A few examples of AI in imaging are as follows:

- Diabetes Care and the first AI approved medical device: In April 2018, the FDA approved the IDx-DR to use AI to detect greater than a mild level of the eye disease, i.e. diabetic retinopathy in adults who have diabetes.[13] This condition occurs when high levels of blood sugar leads to damage in the blood vessels of the retina and is the leading cause of vision impairment among adults.

  The IDx-DR device uses an AI algorithm to analyze images of the eye taken with the Topcon NW400 camera. A physician uploads the digital images of the patient's retinas to a cloud server on which IDx-DR software is installed. The software provides the physician with one of two results: (1) "more than mild diabetic retinopathy detected: refer to an eye care professional" or (2) "negative for more than mild diabetic retinopathy; rescreen in 12 months". If a positive result is detected, patients should see an eye care provider for further evaluation and possible treatment. IDx-DR is the first device authorized for marketing that provides a screening decision without the need for a clinician to interpret the image or results, thereby making it usable by healthcare providers who may not normally be involved in eye care.

- Radiology: FUJIFILM medical systems, a leading provider of Enterprise Imaging and Medical Informatics solutions, and developer of REiLI AI launched a pilot project for chest radiography and mammography imaging.[14] The pilot project is in joint collaboration with Lunit Inc., a Korean-based medical AI software company, and Salud Digna, one of the largest diagnostic service providers in Mexico with 94 clinics around 24 states. The objective of the pilot project is to obtain feedback and input from approximately 20 radiologists at Salud Digna with the long-term goal of advancing the development of AI applications and technologies of both Fujifilm and Lunit. The project also seeks to evaluate worklist prioritization features based on AI solution results, which are intended to improve radiologists' productivity as well as the speed and accuracy of diagnosis.

- Skin Care: The Neutrogena Skin360™ app uses your smartphone to tap into dermatologist-grade technology to analyze your face and show changes over time.[15] The Skin360 software uses AI to track your skin's progress over time and to give you deep information about your skin's actual needs and health. Consumers can now make better informed decisions in choosing the right skincare products vs. choosing a product over the counter.

There are two parts to the innovation; the Skin360 app and a tool called the skin scanner. The skin scanner is fit over the top of your smartphone, magnifies your phone's camera lens and enhances the magnification with eight high-powered LED lights. It also has a "moisture meter" in the form of a ring around the lens that reads hydration levels below the skin's surface. The data and high-resolution images are then transmitted via Bluetooth from the skin scanner to the Neutrogena Skin360 phone app. Using your dermatological data, the app produces an analysis of your skin and ranks it on a scale of 0–100, taking into consideration factors like your age and geographical location. It then further breaks down your score into these core focus areas: moisture, pores, fine lines, and wrinkles. And all of this takes just a few minutes!

AI in Hearing Aids

Starkey Hearing Technologies, the largest manufacturer of hearing aids in the United States and one of the largest in the industry, recently introduced Livio AI, a new class of multi-functional hearing aids with embedded sensors and AI.[16]

"Livio AI is the first-ever hearing aid device that uses built-in sensors and machine learning algorithms to double up as a physical and cognitive activity tracker, a heart-rate measurement device, and an automatic fall detector and alert system", said Dr. Achin Bhowmik, chief technology officer and executive vice president of Starkey. "Furthermore, with connectivity to the smartphone and the cloud, Livio AI is also the first hearing aid in the world that taps into the power of artificial intelligence to provide in-ear language translation, speech transcription, as well as a virtual assistant that responds to gentle taps on the ear and delivers answers to questions asked, privately into the ear, and acoustically compensated for the wearer's hearing loss spectrum".

As seen in this case, the use of AI in hearing aids delivers capabilities that far surpass a traditional product and improves the life of the user. This revolutionary product has been hailed by the press as a category-reshaping step, which could potentially remove some of the stigma that is associated with the traditional assistive devices that limit their broad adoption.[17]

AI in Robotic Surgeries

Robotic surgery is an advanced form of minimally invasive surgery where surgeons use a computer-controlled robot to assist them in certain surgical procedures. The age of surgical AI has commenced with several providers claiming to provide a number of benefits for both the patient and the physician using robotic surgery.[18] Benefits include more precise surgeries, lesser pain, reduced infection, etc. for patients and better dexterity, superior view of operating area, etc. for the physician.

Using AI and data from previous operations, these robotic surgery devices could make better informed surgical techniques.

- Intuitive surgical is a leader in this field, and their devices have been involved in 5 million+ minimally invasive surgeries.[19]
- A study that involved 379 orthopedic patients found that an AI-assisted robotic surgery technique by Mazor Robotics resulted in a reduction of surgical complications to five-fold compared to when surgeons operate alone.[20] The analysis found that when the AI-assisted robotic surgery is applied properly, it could generate a 21% reduction in the patients stay at the hospital as a result of fewer complications and create $40 billion in annual savings.

Predictive Servicing for Medical Equipment

Service contracts have long been one of the most profitable lines of business for medical device equipment manufacturers. The service business margins are much higher than margins from sales of medical equipment. Medical devices are now embedding sensors in the equipment which record anything from operating settings, environmental conditions, adverse events, to faults. With this data they are able to obtain insight into the optimal functioning of the equipment. Applying machine learning algorithms (which is a branch of AI) to this data, medical equipment manufacturers are able to predict failure of the equipment and take corrective actions. These predictive capabilities help to further improve margins for the service business.

We will now look at a few examples of companies that have implemented predictive service.

- Stryker's Smart Equipment Management is designed to help optimize the management of Stryker's smart devices.[21] This solution helps with proactive device maintenance, balanced product use, asset tracking, simplified service, etc.
- GE Healthcare's OnWatch helps minimize unplanned disruptions of medical imaging systems.[22] The technology remotely monitors various imaging system parameters and sends alerts to online service engineers regarding potential errors or the need to take corrective action.
- The Ortho Clinical Diagnostics Predictive Technologies Center (PTC) connects instruments and highly skilled technical support to monitor the performance of the equipment.[23] The PTC is the first of its kind in the in vitro (*process performed in a test tube or dish*) diagnostics industry and provides the potential to reduce downtime and helps to reduce lab downtime.

Silicon Valley's Foray into Medical Devices

Silicon valley's foray into the medical devices industry has begun and we could very soon see some disruptions in this space. In fact, we are already using devices that provide various health monitoring-related functions.

- Smartphones: the average smartphone now can track the number of steps you have walked and your physical activity. The increasing amount of data collected by the smartphones could be used by AI to help recommend healthy routines and predict health outcomes.
- Smart watches: In 2018, the Apple Watch became the first Apple device to be cleared by the FDA and is turning into a serious medical device with fall detection and three heart monitoring capabilities: low heart rate, heart rhythm detection, and a personal electrocardiogram (ECG) monitor.[24] The capabilities on the Apple Watch can indicate whether your heart is showing signs of atrial fibrillation, which is a serious form of irregular heart rhythm. Electrodes built into the digital crown and the back-crystal work together with the ECG app to read your heart's electrical signals.[25]

With the massive amounts of personal health data being captured, the day will soon be here when AI could possibly predict adverse health events and automatically trigger medical help. Medical help from your primary healthcare provider could arrive at your location and in the interim could also possibly crowdsource medical help sending notifications to qualified physicians in close vicinity.

In addition to these devices, several partnerships are being formed by traditional medical device manufacturers and the high-tech software companies. Bringing together software technology expertise like AI and medical device manufacturing expertise can be a powerful combination. An example of such an alliance is Verb Surgical. Verb Surgical is a collaboration by Verily (Verily is an Alphabet company; Alphabet owns Google) and Ethicon (a division of Johnson & Johnson's Medical devices unit).[26] Ethicon brings their deep knowledge of surgery and expertise in surgical instrumentation to this partnership, Verily brings its expertise in data analytics, visualization, and machine learning (a branch of AI) to the verb platform.

AI's Impact on Humanity

AI in medical devices could possibly bring in an era where implanted devices react to minute changes, autonomous surgical systems that operate without direct human involvement, and software in the devices predicting a wide variety of health outcomes. We have already started to see a few examples emerge. There are certainly exciting possibilities; however, we have to keep in mind that as with any new technology there might be some concerns that come to light only during real-life use of the device.

In 2018, a STAT news report suggested that IBM's Watson for Oncology often returned "multiple examples of unsafe and incorrect treatment recommendations".[27] IBM has pushed back stating evidence from use of Watson at several hospitals have provided positive outcomes.[28] While the results could be debated, there is no doubt that patient safety has to be of utmost importance. As the medical devices industry adopts AI and such devices become mainstream, we could possibly see a few cases where the capability does not live up to the hype. Scenarios that AI models have not been trained on, misinterpretation of the results of the AI engine, etc. could lead to challenges in adoption of such devices.

There is no doubt that AI in medical devices can help patients improve their health and provide easier and more convenient means to provide care. Care providers using AI-powered devices would be able to diagnose complex situations faster and provide better outcomes for their patients. The day-to-day care of patients either at a care provider or by means of self-help using a medical device could empower patients to live independently much longer. As these medical devices become increasingly intelligent, we could start living in a world where all living beings are able to stretch our physiological capabilities, symptoms are diagnosed much earlier, and even the onset of a disease could be predicted and averted. These intelligent devices when adopted in masse could significantly help humanity lead better, healthier, and happier lives. The future with AI-enabled medical devices holds a lot of promise!

Notes

1 www.adctoday.com/learning-center/about-stethoscopes/history-stethoscope.
2 www.reportlinker.com/p05380672/Medical-Device-Market-Report-Trends-Forecast-and-Competitive-Analysis.html.
3 www.selectusa.gov/medical-technology-industry-united-states.
4 www.nia.nih.gov/sites/default/files/2017-06/global_health_aging.pdf.
5 www.fda.gov/MedicalDevices/DigitalHealth/ucm55766.htm.
6 www.fda.gov/MedicalDevices/DigitalHealth/ucm575766.htm.
7 www.fda.gov/downloads/Drugs/DevelopmentApprovalProcess/Small BusinessAssistance/UCM466473.pdf.
8 www.congress.gov/bill/114th-congress/house-bill/34/text#toc-H73E766CC 72AC4EB8AAF36670EB540164.
9 www.fda.gov/downloads/MedicalDevices/DeviceRegulationandGuidance/ GuidanceDocuments/UCM587819.pdf.
10 www.fda.gov/MedicalDevices/DigitalHealth/default.htm.
11 www.fda.gov/MedicalDevices/DigitalHealth/SoftwareasaMedicalDevice/ default.htm.
12 www.fda.gov/MedicalDevices/DigitalHealth/DigitalHealthPreCertProgram/ default.htm.

13 www.fda.gov/NewsEvents/Newsroom/PressAnnouncements/ucm604357.htm.
14 www.fujifilmusa.com/press/news/display_news?newsID=881559.
15 www.jnj.com/innovation/neutrogena-skin360-the-revolutionary-face-scanning-device-and-beauty-app.
16 www.starkey.com/hearing-aids/technologies/livio-artificial-intelligence-hearing-aids.
17 http://spectrum.ieee.org/the-human-os/biomedical/devices/starkeys-ai-transforms-hearing-aid-into-smart-wearables.
18 www.mayoclinic.org/tests-procedures/robotic-surgery/about/pac-20394974.
19 www.intuitive.com/en-us/about-us/company.
20 https://hbr.org/2018/05/10-promising-ai-applications-in-health-care.
21 www.stryker.com/us/en/surgical/services/smart-equipment-management.html.
22 www.gehealthcare.com/en/services/onwatch.
23 www.orthoclinicaldiagnostics.com/en-us/home/predictive-technologies.
24 www.healthcareitnews.com/news/apple-unveils-watch-series-4-fda-approved-ecg.
25 www.apple.com/apple-watch-series-4/health/.
26 www.verbsurgical.com/about/our-history/#subnavstart.
27 www.statnews.com/2018/07/25/ibm-watson-recommended-unsafe-incorrect-treatments/.
28 www.massdevice.com/ibm-pushes-back-on-negative-watson-health-stories/.

Chapter 10

Artificial Intelligence and Public Policy

Sophie Guetzko

Accenture

Contents

Overview

The deployment of Artificial Intelligence (AI) and Machine Learning in non-profit organizations (NPOs) and non-governmental organizations (NGOs) is on the rise. Implementation of "smart" technology to routine processes and data analytic insights assists these organizations in financial management, fundraising, and charitable efforts. Addressing potential impacts associated with the adoption of new technology is critical for the deployment of new technology to be successful in organizations.

Nonprofits

Many individuals in America are familiar with the term nonprofit organization (NPO), but may not be as familiar with the requirements that make an organization an NPO. NPOs create awareness and support for a variety of different topics. Some of the most commonly recognized include those for health, poverty, and church organizations. They typically address local issues, but may address national issues. NPOs include any "group organized for purposes other than creating profit" (CMU, n.d.).

They are tax-exempt groups under the Internal Revenue Code section 501(c) (3), Title 26 of the United States Code (U.S.C). There are 29 types of NPOs and may include corporations, community chests, funds, or foundations. The establishment of the organization defines eight purposes, including religious, charitable, testing for public safety, literary or educational, national or international sports competition, and prevention of cruelty to children or animals (26 U.S.C § 501, 2018).

There are two main types of NPOs. The two defined in the 501(c)(3) of the 26 U.S.C defines nonprofits as public charities or private foundations (26 U.S.C § 501, 2018). A public charity is a broadly recognized organization that functions to support another charity or is devoted to testing for public safety. Many rely on donations from the general public. A private foundation is an organization established by a single source of funding, such as an individual, family, or corporate money. While donations to private foundations are tax deductible, many do not accept donations, as if they were created on investment income and have specified tax requirements that must be followed (IRS, 2018).

Non-Governmental Organizations

While many NGOs are NPOs, not as many NPOs are NGOs. Similar in acronym but different in establishment, an NGO is "any nonprofit, voluntary citizens group which is organized on a local, national, or international level" (NGO.org, 2018). An NGO typically operates independent of government influence, but they may receive government funding. The phrase is not typically used when referring to US-based NPOs, but is used in cases where the impact of the organization is international (GrantSpace, 2018).

The United Nations defines an NGO in the following way: "a not-for profit, voluntary citizen's group that is organized on a local, national or international level to address issues in support of the public good. Task-oriented and made up of people with a common interest, NGOs perform a variety of services and humanitarian functions, bring citizen's concerns to Governments, monitor policy and program implementation, and encourage participation of civil society stakeholders at the community level" (Leverty, 2019).

The actions related to an NGO include work with environments, social, advocate, and human rights. An estimated 15% of overseas development takes place based on NGO involvement, and help with community and societal development (GrantSpace, 2018).

Artificial Intelligence and Machine Learning

AI and Machine Learning are sometimes used interchangeably. However, they are different and hold different purpose in use. AI takes machines we use and enhances them to make them "smart". AI-enabled machines require human interaction to continue enhancements (Marr, 2016).

When thinking AI, consider the voice to text feature on a smartphone, spam filters in email, and personalization of ads in news feeds on social media. In order for AI to be "smart", a user gives data to a machine, the machine processes the data it was provided, and then the machine produces feedback based on the initial command it was given.

Machine Learning takes AI one step further. When a user puts the initial data into the machine, the machine is able to continue to process information and learn connections, processes, and develop "thoughts" around the data that was initially inputted (Marr, 2016).

Examples of Machine Learning include virtual personal assistants, facial recognition on social media platforms and smartphone photo albums, search engine requirement refining, and product recommendations. A user gives data to a machine, the machine processes the data it was provided, the machine produces feedback, and then, the user provides feedback to the machine, which then evaluates its own performance and determines how to meet the needs of a user more effectively in future interactions.

Use of AI and Machine Learning in NPOs and NGOs

The deployment of AI and Machine Learning in organizations is on the rise to manage and respond to routine requests in a variety of industries and impacts. Use of AI in corporations to manage finance, human resources, and communication has also been implemented in NPOs and NGOs.

Donors and Fundraising

Financial management and fraud evaluation is one form of AI and Machine Learning in the workplace today. Financial tools with AI can assist in the detection of actions that require additional evaluation, spot abnormalities in transactions, and identify misconduct in finances. The criticality of effective financial management of NPOs and NGOs is important to the success of the organization.

Fundraising efforts can also be enhanced through the use of AI. The implementation of data analytics alongside the use of user data can assist in targeting people who would have a greater likelihood to donate to the cause. An example of how this data analytics technology can aid in a busy workday would be the ability to generate a massive amount of personalized emails to donors with custom tailored messages based on a number of their previous behaviors. AI quickly collects data and can produce insights that would take a significant amount of time for a human to complete. The ability to provide actionable insights based on data analytics is an asset to NPOs. AI and Machine Learning can often manage and predict individual donations and project the size of the donation based on previous engagements.

Charitable Efforts

The capabilities of AI and Machine Learning are on the rise. The following foundational examples outline some of the growing abilities that AI and Machine Learning possess and will add further value to as they progress throughout the coming years.

By using AI and Machine Learning in the form of data analytics and complex insights it can greatly aid in the pursuit of enhanced disaster relief response. Users are able to ask specific questions to the machines, which can produce coherent insights and feedback from real-world situations with complex data. In September 2007 following Hurricane Maria, an estimated 10,000 containers containing relief supplies was sitting idle while disaster relief officials coordinated distribution efforts. Due to a surplus of data, experts are still diagnosing best practice in what data to use, when it should be used, and how it should be used in data relief efforts (Catlin, 2018).

In the past, detectives operated on a scarcity of data; today, it is quite the opposite. In a similar case to disaster relief, excess of data in the instances of crime resolution – sorting the data that is important, and the data that is not – is an ongoing development in the area of human trafficking prevention and rescue of trafficked individuals. Thorn, a charity founded by Ashton Kutcher, has developed an algorithm to sort data and track important data. Traffickers often post advertisements online, but use varying email addresses and phone numbers, so it is difficult to track.

Law enforcement officials and others working in human trafficking recovery organizations often manually review the advertisements online, but the time it takes to sort, review, and action on the data collected limits the impact in recovery efforts. In cases like these, Machine Learning can be implemented to recognize and learn patterns in language, images, and identify suspects at a faster rate than a human can perform. However, like most things, this ability to sort and track has downfalls as well. Authorities may identify individuals who are undercover for legitimate reasons (Accenture UK, 2018).

Virtual personal assistants can provide 24/7 support to beneficiaries and donors to access services and discover information. Some Internet of Things (IoT) devices have been enabled to create pathways that direct information along pathways identified by the user, such as the Echo Show smart speaker by Amazon, which allows users to make video calls to one another (Accenture, 2019a).

The introduction of chatbots in customer service has the capacity to elevate the customer service experience. The ability to hold real-time conversations with humans 24/7, answer questions with little to no wait time, and work as a donation platform has created a positive impact. The charitable jewelry brand Lokai and nonprofit charity: water was able to raise awareness about the water crisis by walking customers through a story of an individual's experience in retrieving daily water. The chatbot was provided through Facebook Messenger (Accenture, 2019a).

Potential Impacts of AI and Machine Learning for NPOs and NGOs

Increased distribution, accessibility, and advancements in technology, as well as demand for service, allow space for AI and Machine Learning to appear as a best path, best practice initiative for organizations looking to keep up in a data-driven world. The good that AI and Machine Learning can provide is and will continue to enhance everyday life. However, like most things, there are potential impacts that drive value away from the implementation of new technology. Use of AI and Machine Learning requires change management principles and vigilance to ensure value creation.

Based on survey data, 47% of people want to make their contribution to charity via digital platforms. Sixty-one percent of people think nonprofits should use more digital technology. On average, 42% of people would donate greater than or equal to 10% more if a personalized experience is provided, which increases to 62% for millennials (Accenture Public Service Global Citizen Survey, 2017).

NPOs and NGOs may feel an increased pressure to meet the demands from donors and beneficiaries to continue to drive fundraising efforts in a digital-driven world. Global Management Consulting and Professional Services firm Accenture recommends four ways to assess the present challenges and transform them into opportunities (Accenture, 2019b):

Reframe Strategy and Operations. Development or revision of a written strategic plan assists in the framework toward the implementation or advancement of technology in an organization. Suggested process is to begin by mapping the strategy to move the organization forward, build, and equip your workforce, streamline your operations, and communicate effectively with your stakeholders.

Magnify Results through Analytics. Less than 4 in 10 nonprofits have implemented use of data analytics. For the ~4% who have, 83% report significant gains in efficiency. Data analytics help NPOs accessing relevant data, share insights, and collaborate (Accenture Public Service Global Citizen Survey, 2017).

Captivate Digital Constituent. Communication to donors and beneficiaries assists in trust development and overall impact. An estimated 80% of citizens consider it important to know the impact of donations and volunteer work. In addition, 44% would be willing to give greater than or equal to 10% more for an experience that is personalized to them. Having a data-driven approach, telling a story, and audience engagement on a variety of platforms can assist in developing and enhancing donor relationships and leveraging those relationships to maintain consistency in giving.

Accelerate Impact Through Technology. Insufficient service delivery and legacy infrastructure can create obstacles in a nonprofit's ability to introduce AI and Machine Learning. Making updates to IT strategy, integrating systems that are not working together, use of cloud and other IT solutions, and growth of technology-enabled ecosystems have been proven to assist organizations in the nonprofit sector. Nine out of ten nonprofits who have introduced digital accelerators have experience gains in efficiency.

Impacts of technology are often met with challenges. Accenture has identified potential obstacles in the adoption of AI and Machine Learning technologies (Accenture, 2019c):

Cost. Current offerings from vendors are often expensive, even for proof of concept initiatives.

Security of data. The requirement to share personal data and potentially sensitive data with third parties and cloud providers can cause hesitation in some organizations.

Customization and ease of use. Current software-as-a-service (SAAS) offerings are not customizable to meet specific requirements that may be requested by an organization.

Vendor lock-in and future-proofing. AI is a rapidly changing technology. At the present time, choosing a vendor can be a challenging process, and industry and technological changes can take place at a rate that is faster than implementation.

Conclusion

As a whole, the rise of AI in the nonprofit sector initiates a shift that shapes and reshapes organizations, their processes, cost structures, and efforts by revolutionizing the use of technology. Simple adjustments toward AI and Machine Learning opportunities can enhance strategy, business processes, and overall ways of working. These advancements, when implemented properly, create opportunities for growth and impact unmatched by that of competitors who choose to remain stagnant in processes.

References

26 U.S.C § 501. (2018). Retrieved from https://uscode.house.gov/view.xhtml?req=(title: 26%20section:501%20edition:prelim).

Accenture UK. (January 16, 2018). Using Artificial Intelligence to fight human trafficking. Retrieved from www.accenture.com/gb-en/blogs/blogs-using-ai-fight-human-trafficking.

Accenture. (2019a). Emerging trends in the validation of machine learning and artificial intelligence models. Retrieved from www.accenture.com/us-en/insight-emerging-trends-machine-learning.

Accenture. (2019b). Technology on a mission: Together, humans and AI are nonprofit's force for good. Retrieved from https://voicesfrompublicservice.accenture.com/unitedstates/nonprofits-collaborating-with-ai.

Accenture. (2019c). *Getting today's nonprofit right in the digital age.* Retrieved from www.accenture.com/us-en/no-pressure-no-diamonds-nonprofit-index.

Accenture Public Service Global Citizen Survey. (May 2017). *Survey.* Retrieved from www.accenture.com/us-en/no-pressure-no-diamonds-nonprofit-index.

Catlin, J. (December 6, 2018). Artificial intelligence for disaster relief: A primer. Retrieved from www.lexalytics.com/lexablog/artificial-intelligence-disaster-relief.

CMU. (n.d.). Key differences between non-government organizations (NGO) and nonprofit organizations. Retrieved from www.cmu.edu/career/documents/industry-guides/NGOs%20and%20NPOs.pdf.

GrantSpace. (2018). What is an NGO? What role does it play in civil society? Retrieved from https://grantspace.org/resources/knowledge-base/ngo-definition-and-role/.

IRS. (2018). EO operational requirements: Private foundations and public charities. Retrieved from www.irs.gov/charities-non-profits/eo-operational-requirements-private-foundations-and-public-charities.

Leverty, S. (2019). NGOS, the UN, and APA. Retrieved from https://www.apa.org/international/united-nations/publications.

Marr, B. (Dec 6, 2016). What is the difference between artificial intelligence and machine learning? Retrieved from www.forbes.com/sites/bernardmarr/2016/12/06/what-is-the-difference-between-artificial-intelligence-and-machine-learning/#45a1e2342742.

NGO.org. (2018). Definition of NGOs. Retrieved from www.ngo.org/ngoinfo/define.html.

Chapter 11

Artificial Intelligence in Education

Matthew Lievertz
Zylo

Contents

Introduction

During the early stages of the space race, humans with the job title "Computer" provided many of the calculations necessary for progress (McLennan and Gainer 2012, 26). According to McLennan and Gainer, NASA's predecessor organization purchased an early programmable computer, The Bell Electronic Computer, in 1947 (31), and by the mid-1970s, human computers had disappeared from the organization (26). Yet, if one examines the broader project of space technology, humans did not become obsolete – only the trivial matter of computation is left to machines.

In recent years, professionals in the education space have raised a number of thoughtful questions about the emergence of artificial intelligence (AI).

Will machines replace educators? How will the classroom change? How will institutions change? Beyond these questions, of course it bears mentioning that indeed, like most topics in basic research, many of the foundations and great advances of AI are occurring as a product of higher education research... and then in turn, these advances have started to themselves be utilized in other areas and avenues of research (e.g., genomics, financial modeling, chemical analysis).

This chapter will not provide a comprehensive treatment of all of these questions and aspects. Deep insight into the frontiers of research is best reserved for academic literature in the various research fields themselves. The institutional impact of AI on education for schools, universities, etc. will be profound, but should have close parallels to the impact of AI on other large organizations (for which the reader can utilize other chapters in this book). Instead, this chapter will focus on ways that AI will transform the educational process itself: teaching, learning, the classroom, and the student and educator experiences in the near and mid-term. Much broader and less predictable changes are likely beyond the next decade. This chapter focuses on the more practical and discernable changes that can be anticipated in the coming decade.

Coming back around to the historical metaphor heading this chapter, as AI comes into its own as an integrated tool in education in the next decade, it is far more useful to consider the calculator than it is to imagine androids forcing educators into retirement. The calculator, or even the traditional computer more broadly, has been hugely impactful for education, clearly, but the impact has only been to shift educator focus from the rote to the creative. Benedict Evans, a partner at venture-capital firm Andreessen Horowitz, suggests we think about the problems AI will solve in the near future as tasks we could ask a large number of fifteen-year olds to complete (2018). An army of young teenagers could complete so many tasks that non-learning computers struggle to automate – all kinds of tasks requiring a modicum of human sense or vision... Yet, this unruly army still ought to follow the judicious direction of a qualified adult, who will provide guidance and re-enforcement. In other words, AI is going to have a huge impact on education, but it will be through the introduction of powerful new tools and capabilities, not the replacement of educators.

In seeking to characterize the impact of AI on education in the next decade, this chapter looks to the confluence of relevant major trends in education with major new technological capabilities enabled by AI. These educational trends include increases in:

■ The role and prevalence of distance/online/distributed learning (Becker et al. 2018, Wilson et al. 2014),
■ Demand for personalized education and other solutions to enrollment/class size pressure (Becker et al. 2018, Wilson et al. 2014), and
■ Accountability for educational outcomes (Becker et al. 2018, Wilson et al. 2014).

The first-order technological capabilities enabled by AI include:

■ Natural language processing (NLP) (the ability of computers to correctly utilize non-structured inputs like free-responses) (Young et al. 2018),
■ Computer/machine vision (the ability of computers to process photo/video inputs in useful ways, such as identifying what is in a picture, or understanding the movement of people in frame) (Kahn et al. 2019),
■ Visual generation (the ability of computers to generate or adapt static or moving visualizations that have not been explicitly pre-programmed) (Jenal et al. 2019) (the well-known Pokemon Go smartphone game is an example of augmented reality (AR), which is powered by visual generation) (Hanke 2018),
■ Translation (the ability of computers to accurately translate information from one format or language to another. Text-to-speech is an example of format translation) (Lee, Kim, and Lee 2018, Laubli, Sennrich, and Volk 2018), and
■ Machine learning (the ability of computers to, based on large amounts of data, create insightful models for use in predictions, classification, matching, etc.) (Sambasivan, Das, and Sahu 2018).

The remainder of this chapter will explore specific applications of the above in the teaching and learning space.

Time-Savings for Educators

Feedback from the educator to the pupil is a critical and valued part of the educational process, but for maximum effectiveness should be specific, timely, and linked to learning objectives (Higgins, Hartley, and Skelton 2002, 56–60, Goodwin and Miller 2012, Schinske and Tanner 2014). At the same time, feedback takes considerable time and will take more time as the size of classrooms continues to increase (Nicol and MacFarlane-Dick 2006, 201). According to a 2012 time use study, teachers spent greater than 20% of a nearly 9-h average day on assessment grading (DePaepe 2014). In specific circumstances such as essay grading, educators may spend extraordinary lengths of time – one educator blogs a detailed account of just under 32 h spent grading 78 persuasive essays (Zerwin 2011). Time and quality clearly fight for primacy here, and the educational trends of larger class sizes and demand for more personalization would only exacerbate the conflict. Fortunately, many emergent AI applications aim squarely at providing both educators and pupils with timely and time-saving feedback.

One straightforward feature AI enables is the broadening of automatically gradable inputs. NLP enables computers to assign meaning to free textual responses. Discernable meanings include sentiment analysis, part-of-speech analysis, and semantic meaning and classification (Young et al. 2018). Using NLP, assessment applications such as learning management systems (LMS) and other course and assessment software could weigh the acceptability of a short response without a comprehensive answer bank, instead learning on a large knowledge base and/or a sample answer bank provided by the educator (similar to research discussed by Young et al. 2018 on pages 9 and 20). The software could compute a probability that the answer is correct. Above a configurable upper bound, the software auto-grades the response as "correct", and similarly below a configurable lower bound, the software auto-grades "incorrect". It is likely that in many applications, and increasingly as the technology progresses, that all question responses can be handled automatically. As technology and adoption matures, however, unclear responses between the upper and lower bounds could be returned to the grader with suggested grades, and the grader could validate or correct those suggestions.

Timely Student Feedback and Plagiarism Detection

A number of products currently on the market already take the suggestion approach using advanced text analytics together with NLP and machine learning to provide students and educators with plagiarism detection, metrics, and evaluative feedback on written responses such as essays or message board contributions. Among the best-known providers of these services, Turnitin offers products that evaluate originality (Feedback Studio) (2019a) and provide automated feedback on length, proofing, claim clarity, support strength, organization, and language use (Revision Assistant) (2019b). The purchasing institution can enable either of these tools for independent student use. Interestingly, Turnitin also provides a student-as-direct-customer product called WriteCheck (2017), providing support for the concept that this kind of automated, timely feedback holds market-tested value. Another major automated feedback provider is Blackboard, which offers features on its LMS products to detect plagiarism (SafeAssign) (Blackboard 2019) and several feedback analytics features (X-ray and discussion analysis) providing insight into discussion participation, linguistic complexity (Blackboard 2018a, b), and an attempt to capture critical thinking (Blackboard 2018a). Grammarly provides a licensed institutional product, but prominently offers its services directly to consumers (Grammarly 2019a). Grammarly's core product is a plagiarism checker (2019c), but its premium offering also includes proofing and style feedback (Grammarly 2019a).

Data on the effectiveness of the above plagiarism detection products point to the importance of machine learning and NLP to maturing this product category. Several studies found significant gaps in the ability of TurnItIn and SafeAssign (these market leaders have received the majority of critical study) to identify large blocks of purposefully plagiarized control text. In Schorn's 2007 test, these products found only 43%–61% of plagiarized control text, and she replicated her findings with TurnItIn (found 40%–56%) in 2015. Hunt and Tompkins' 2014 test showed the products to find only 55%–64% of the plagiarized control texts (71). Walchuk's 2016 test showed TurnItIn to find 71% of the plagiarized control texts (48–52), and he highlighted the fact that the majority of missed material came from the oldest sources in the control texts (articles from 1970, 1976, and 1982) (34). These omissions are concerning primarily because 100% of the control texts were known plagiarized material, highlighting the concept that data access is and will remain paramount despite technological advances. Several researchers note that semantic-level plagiarism may go entirely undetected (Schorn 2015, Vrbanec and Mestovic 2017, Walchuk 2016, 34) – an indication that usage of NLP and machine learning in these products is as-of-yet immature. Plagiarism detection through semantic similarity is an active area of research (Vrbanec and Mestovic 2017), however, so it is likely that these advances will find their way into these products in the near and/to mid-term.

Case studies utilizing the above products for automated student feedback provided a consistent and far more positive message: automated student feedback was useful as an independent learning tool (Biggam and McCann 2010, Mills n.d.), especially valuable when used as a reference-point for educator-led feedback (Coast 2016), and in some cases enabled educators to tackle advanced concepts after students learned mechanics through the automated feedback (Straumsheim 2016). Grammarly claims that users report increased writing enjoyment (76%), writing strength improvements (85%), and writing grade improvements (99%) in user surveys ("Grammarly Premium" 2019a). These initial findings support the idea that this type of feedback product may improve learning outcomes, though rigorous study on the topic is lacking.

There is good reason to suspect that machine learning enabled by NLP would be able to provide useful feedback on writing, however. For instance, Pezdek suggests a methodology (largely aimed at improving the efficiency of human grading) which identifies specific recurring feedback categories such as transition difficulties, casual style, or redundant language (2009). This type of category identification is exactly the sort of problem at which machine learning excels: identify this pattern, and highlight and tag text areas where it occurs. Over time, usage of data would reinforce the usefulness of this feedback, and indeed, this appears to be what TurnItIn's Revision Assistant (Newton 2017) and Grammarly Premium aim to do (Grammarly 2019b, "Spotlight"). These rapid-feedback tools enable and inspire students to engage in more iterations and learn many of the basic concepts on their own, guided by the feedback software, and this promotes writing improvement and enables instructors to spend time on advanced concepts (Straumsheim 2016).

Enhanced Feedback and Personalization

Just as machine learning may excel at identifying common writing problem patterns, machine learning can be applied to identify common failure patterns in mathematics, science, or other "show your work" situations. For homework, students could receive feedback *as they are exhibiting a mistake pattern* and quickly learn to identify and correct it (e.g., a pop-up that says "Whoops! Check your units!"). For graded work, the software could help educators identify common failure patterns (e.g., student A's work exhibits the pattern of accidentally missing a sign reversal in an algebra problem, but was otherwise correct) so as to provide more targeted feedback and/or award partial credit.

These capabilities are related to an educational strategy called adaptive or personalized learning. The Association of Public Land Trust Universities' Personalized Learning Consortium (APLU PLC) members released a series of reports (from participating member universities) with a subheading entitled "Moving from Scaling to Sustainable" demonstrating that adoption of this new technology is well underway among leading higher education institutions (e.g., Carter 2018, Johnson 2018, Luke 2018, Tesene 2018). Most universities reported working with three to four vendors [O'Sullivan reports the highest number, nine, at the University of Mississippi (2018) – only one university reported less than three, with two at the University of Oregon (Greenwood 2018)]; most reports list four to six participating courses, but at the higher end Buchan reports 15 courses at Colorado State University (2018), and O'Sullivan reports 18 courses at the University of Mississippi; and perhaps most impressive are counts of enrolled students, ranging from a low of 1,424 students at Portland State University (De Gruyter and Berg 2018) to a high of 6,017 students at the University of Mississippi (O'Sullivan 2018). These reports show far more than pilot adoption impacting the learning experiences of thousands of students.

Within the broad heading of adaptive learning, product capabilities range in diversity and on a spectrum. EdSurge published a widely cited report in 2016 attempting to define and categorize capabilities on this spectrum:

- Adaptive content refers to the capability to provide feedback to student responses beyond correct/incorrect, such as indicating what kind of mistake was made and/or providing relevant supplementary or review material to help improve student understanding of the content;
- Adaptive assessment refers to the capability to dynamically alter assessment interactions as a student responds – the system uses responses to change what questions the student sees after that point (e.g., perhaps making future questions more or less difficult, or adjusting question topics after the student has shown evidence of mastery or non-mastery the current topic); and
- Adaptive sequence refers to a capability set wherein the system uses a student's cumulative interaction history to make decisions about the selection, timing, format, and depth of content to deliver and assess.

The range of products and capabilities in this space can be well understood by understanding the above typology against a conceptual architecture of how vendors can deliver these capabilities. Howlin and Lynch provide an adaptive learning system framework consisting of (1) content – which could be essentially the same content that digital courses today utilize; (2) curriculum – "regular" courses have a curriculum already, but either a course author will need to input it into the system by hand-designing a sequence, or the curriculum will need to utilize a machine-readable structure (such as various types of network graphs that embody prerequisites and dependencies); (3) learner – here the authors discuss either a course-author-supplied learner profile (e.g., student A is a tactile learner with a 3.4 GPA) or a profile that the system constructs based on learner interactions; and (4) an engine that utilizes the prior elements to provide an adaptive learning experience for the learner (2014).

Looking at the most basic adaptive content capability, such a system (which only provides enhanced feedback to student responses) provides responses from content to the engine, which may in turn provide other content in response. Note that the curriculum and learner profile portions of the conceptual architecture are not necessarily implemented in this system. That does not necessarily mean that an adaptive content capability is not complex. The enhanced feedback the system provides could be as simple as grammar checking (e.g., as is common in word processing applications today), but could also implement innovative machine learning algorithms to provide relevant feedback to complex problem areas (e.g., a hypothetical system might critique the design of a proposed experiment in biology).

The next capability in the spectrum, adaptive assessment, implies the addition of the learner profile and/or the curriculum, so that the engine has a basis on which to decide how to adapt an assessment. For instance, a system may model a student's demonstrated skill level to provide later questions chosen to match that level; or, a system may utilize a curriculum graph that allows the system to efficiently establish knowledge of content areas because the system knows that once competency is shown in topic C, the student is likely to also be competent in prerequisite topics A and B (this prerequisite relationship being established by the curriculum graph).

Finally, the last capability set in the spectrum, adaptive sequencing, implies a full implementation of the conceptual architecture. The engine utilizes content which is keyed to a curriculum graph, informed by a (constantly improving) learner profile, to deliver a highly personalized learning experience. One leading adaptive learning vendor, SmartSparrow, draws a distinction here between "designed adaptivity" – where the engine's decision-points are manually built by instructional designers – and "algorithmic adaptivity" – where the engine uses AI to act as a completely individualized (but non-human) instructional designer (2018). SmartSparrow appears to utilize designed adaptivity with an extensive, AI-powered toolset for enhanced feedback, adaptive assessment, and learner profiling, but allows/requires educators to make professional, human decisions about how to design content sequences based on and utilizing this toolset (Ben-Naim 2017, Ben-Naim, Marcus, and Bain 2008).

One vendor with an AI-powered engine is Cerego, which utilizes a model structured around knowledge retention and a learner profile built around the attributes of knowledge, diligence, and agility (Harlow 2018). Based on the learner profile attributes, the engine designs a learning sequence around short, interspersed lessons – at each lesson, the learner practices knowledge retrieval, and the practice of knowledge retrieval, in the Cerego pedagogical model, is associated with long-term retention (Harlow, Mumma, and Lewis 2016). Realizeit, another vendor with an AI-powered engine, uses a more traditional pedagogical model that begins with an adaptive assessment of existing learner knowledge (Lynch and Howlin 2014). The Realizeit system utilizes a classification system for different content types and tracks effectiveness of these types against learner profiles in addition to tracking predicted learner ability for concepts in the curriculum (Howlin 2018). As the student proceeds in the course, the engine continually attempts to match the learner with the content that best matches that learner's pre-existing knowledge, learning style, and ability (Howlin 2018).

Looking at the structure of AI-engine-driven adaptive learning solutions, one can imagine a next step where students can have supplementary interactions with an AI-powered helper entity – a virtual tutor that can interact using natural language, provide answers to ad hoc questions, and perhaps provide supplementary information for the curious student who wants to know more. This could be implemented as an expert system, which is an AI that aims to approximate human judgment in a subject area, primarily through use of advanced input and output capabilities (such as natural language processing and generation) around a knowledge base and inference engine (e.g., IBM's Watson) (Azati 2018, Boss, 1991).

Note that while existing vendors largely provide an application-based solution, one of the educational technology subcurrents that has persisted since 2015 has been an awareness of a transition from application-focus (e.g., LMS) to a platform-focus (e.g., the Next Generation Digital Learning Environment, or NGDLE) (EDUCAUSE 2019, Miller and Duan 2018). As Miller and Duan report, an existing implementation of this pattern by the University of Notre Dame accesses student activity data in industry-standard formats (e.g., xAPI or CALIPER) from different source applications and can then provide useful analytics of student behavior (2018). This architectural pattern can easily be imagined to extend to a machine learning services – as ever, educational institutions are wise to maintain an eye on open standards use and vendor capabilities to evolve into future architectural paradigms, especially because the content-production requirements for any kind of digital course, especially with adaptive learning, are weighty.

Matching Benefits and Hazards

As noted in the section on adaptive learning, many educational AI vendors have begun creating learner profiles. Carrying this concept forward to AI-powered interpersonal, institutional, and employer matching brings forward great potential, but also special hazards. As it turns out, a machine decision-maker does not guarantee objectivity: AI may exhibit systemic bias, raising significant ethical and practical concerns if personal characteristics are brought to bear on decision-making. Caliskan, Bryson, and Narayanan showed that standard machine learning techniques aimed at a standard written corpus (the Google News corpus) would exhibit expected racial and gender stereotypes, showing clearly that where there are stereotypes present in a data set, those stereotypes may persist in a machine learning model trained on that data set (2017).

Villasenor notes an additional source of bias: some data has correlative links (e.g., race and zip code), and even when these are accounted for in a specific application of machine learning, it is possible that a later iteration of that algorithm could fail to consider biased indirect factors that are no longer corrected (2019). IBM reports over 180 specific human biases it is tracking in an attempt to combat AI bias before AI bias undermines public confidence in AI (IBM 2019) and yet, the sheer number of biases at play speak to the difficulty of addressing this problem, which may be intractable.

AI bias has frustrated numerous real-world attempts to use AI to make decisions about individuals. Angwin et al. found that a criminal sentencing recommendation engine was nearly twice as likely to incorrectly label a black defendant (44.9%) as high risk when there was no re-offense versus a white defendant (23.5%), and that the engine made nearly the exact reverse mistake in incorrectly labeling white defendants as low risk when they did re-offend (47.7%) versus black defendants (28.0%) (2016). Levin reports an incident where Beauty.AI, a company with an AI intended to objectively judge human beauty, held a beauty contest where over 6,000 participants from 100 countries were narrowed down to 44 winners, of whom nearly all were white (2016). In 2014, Amazon started building an AI-powered recruiting engine, but in 2015 concluded it was systemically discriminating against female candidates (Dastin 2018). The company attempted to correct for this discrimination for 2 years before executives finally pulled the plug because they could not be certain that the AI would not be discriminatory (Dastin 2018).

Given the significant risks, why pursue AI-powered matching at all? There are a number of possible benefits if the ethical and practical hazards could be dealt with. Educator-student and student-section fit can have huge implications on educational outcomes as well as perceived student (customer) and educator (employee) satisfaction. Educators could also harness AI matching to better control the risk factors of student group work – groups that were more conducive to learning could be selected, and/or educators might be pre-warned about potential problem students or groups and have the capability to keep a closer eye or provide a timely intervention. AI matching might also enable currently underutilized interpersonal solutions such as recommending compatible study partners or tutors. On the institutional level, AI matching could improve admissions to programs and institutions and provide a leg-up when seeking to place students with companies for internships or employment. As noted, the technology is presently immature and unproven in this very thorny area. These types of solutions are worth keeping an eye on to ensure rigorous evaluation when they emerge, but also to be aware of the huge benefits if they pass muster.

One narrow use case where this type of application has succeeded are early warning systems, which are designed to identify students at risk of negative educational outcomes so that institutions can provide timely interventions and avoid the negative outcome. Purdue University implemented one of the first of these systems with a pilot in 2007 and broad adoption in 2009 (Tally 2009). Arnold and Pistilli reported in 2012 that courses using signals saw an average increase in As and Bs of 10.37%, and an average decrease in Ds and Fs of 6.41%, as compared to the same courses prior to using the system. Since then, vendor offerings and institution adoptions in the product category have grown rapidly. The National Forum on Educational Statistics reports that approximately half of public high schools used a system like this as of the 2014–2015 academic year (2018).

Format Barriers and Immersion

Another way of personalizing education is to provide flexibility in content and course delivery formats. There are a number of existing products that use machine learning as the engine behind the ability to translate material and delivery between formats. This is exceptionally useful for accessibility, and accessibility currently drives the market impetus in this area, but like most accessibility issues, nearly everyone stands to benefit. The popularity of audiobooks and podcasts illustrates the context-sensitive nature of how individuals prefer to get content. AI will enable the near-seamless translation of content, produced once in the educator's preferred format, to any consumption format desired by the student – text, audio, and even video.

Course delivery will also stand to benefit from AI-powered applications in virtual reality (VR – immersive media that brings the user into a computer-facilitated or generated virtual experience, which relies on machine learning to power construction of immersive media) and augmented reality (AR – media that brings computer-facilitated or computer-generated virtual elements or overlays into interaction with the real world, which relies on computer vision as the connection-point between the virtual and real). VR technologies can be used to provide an immersive in-class experience for distance education students. This may also have physical classroom impacts. As distance students participating in real-time VR becomes commonplace, it may become normal to include a classroom avatar, providing a point-source for distance student voices and possibly even animating student likeness (which, from the perspective of the physical classroom, would be a use of AR). AI-powered video processing could construct virtual classrooms that knit a group of distance participants into a single, live, virtual visual, and audio space. This may provide great enhancements for distance learning quality, and in turn may further increase the prevalence of this trend.

VR and AR can also be used to give students completely new kinds of experiences. An example VR application would be to construct curated, cut-to-time, inexpensive field trips. Architectural history students could virtually tour important historic structures, rather than merely show two-dimensional photos and videos. Reciprocally, AR applications can extend classroom learning beyond the traditional classroom space and time. An example AR application would be a smartphone app that identified architectural features via computer vision and image classification – those same architectural history students could bring their new knowledge and curiosity out of the classroom and continue to be guided and educated about features in their environments.

Paradigm Change

Looking broadly, AI enables software to gain many critical components of basic human intelligence, such as the ability to:

- get meaning from visual inputs,
- get meaning from language,
- recognize categories and patterns, and
- make predictive models.

Many current systems and heuristics – large portions of our present conception of how the world words – rely on assumptions about format, distance, the ability of computer systems to interact with the real world, and the kinds of judgment and predictions that computer system can make – which will become invalid. Many changes in the next decade, especially in the next 5 years, are likely to follow along the lines presented and hinted so far in this chapter.

The speed and potential integration effects of AI-enabled change is such that there is a reasonable likelihood of paradigm change before the next decade is up. The educational paradigm change(s) in the next decade will likely take the form of the extreme amplification of one or more current trends after a bottleneck is removed. As an example, as format barriers fall and latent knowledge assessment improves, distributed learning and democratized credentialing may experience explosive growth, causing corresponding large drops in demand for a traditional university experience and large increases in demand for non-university-affiliated credible educators. That huge, hypothetical paradigm shift would be based on trends that exist today, but at a completely different scale.

One paradigm shift that is clear is that the educator's role will move higher up the value hierarchy. One model of knowledge known as the DIKW Pyramid (data–information–knowledge–wisdom) seeks to provide a framework around this. The basis of knowledge is data (e.g., an observation) upon which information (e.g., a general pattern based on many observations) can be synthesized. Knowledge suggests a useful application of information, e.g., leveraging a general pattern to make a conditional recommendation, or a system of decision-making.

Finally, wisdom represents the highest level of consideration and would perhaps make a critical evaluation of a decision-making system and identify areas and methods of future improvement. In the next decade and beyond, AI will become the most effective teacher for bottom half of the DIKW pyramid: data, information, and basic knowledge. Educators will focus on the top half of the DIKW pyramid: knowledge and wisdom. Students will look to new AI-powered tools for technical skills, but will look to educators for a rich, critical discussion of how these skills fit into life and practice.

References

Angwin, Julia, Jeff Larson, Surya Mattu, and Lauren Kirchner. 2016. "Machine Bias." *ProPublica*. May 23, 2016. Accessed February 5, 2019. www.propublica.org/article/machine-bias-risk-assessments-in-criminal-sentencing.

Arnold, Kimberly E. and Matthew D. Pistilli. "Course Signals at Purdue University: Using Learning Analytics to Increase Student Success." In *Proceedings of the 2nd International Conference on Learning Analytics and Knowledge (LAK'12), Vancouver, British Colombia*, April 29–May 2, 2012. 267–270. doi:10.1145/2330601.2330666.

Azati Software. 2018. "Difference Between Artificial Intelligence and Expert System in 2018." Last Modified May 11, 2018. Accessed January 21, 2019. https://azati.com/the-return-of-expert-systems/.

Becker, Samantha Adams, Malcolm Brown, Eden Dahlstrom, Annie Davis, Kristi DePaul, Veronica Diaz, and Jeffrey Pomerantz. 2018. NCM Horizon Report: *2018 Higher Education Edition*. Louisville, CO: EDUCAUSE, 2018. Accessed January 21, 2019. https://library.educause.edu/~/media/files/library/2018/8/2018horizonreport.pdf.

Ben-Naim, Dror. 2017. "Where are We Going with Learning and Assessment? Educational Technology and Computation Psychometrics Symposium 2017." Last Modified December 19, 2017. Accessed February 5, 2019. www.smartsparrow.com/2017/12/19/where-are-we-going-with-learning-and-assessment-takeaways-from-etcps-2017/.

Ben-Naim, Dror, Nadine Marcus, and Mike Bain. "Visualization and Analysis of Student Interactions in an Adaptive Exploratory Learning Environment." In *European Conference of Technology Enhanced Learning, Maastricht, The Netherlands*, 16–19 September, 2008. http://ftp.informatik.rwth-aachen.de/Publications/CEUR-WS/Vol-381/paper01.pdf.

Biggam, John and Margaret McCann. 2010. "A Study of Turnitin as an Educational Tool in Student Dissertations." *Interactive Technology and Smart Education* 7 no. 1 (2010): 44–54. doi:10.1108/17415651011031644.

Blackboard. 2018a. "Discussions Report." Accessed January 21, 2019. https://help.blackboard.com/Blackboard_Open_LMS/Teacher/Track_Progress/X-Ray_Learning_Analytics/Discussions_Report.

Blackboard. 2018b. "View Discussion Performance and Analytics." Accessed January 21, 2019. https://help.blackboard.com/Learn/Instructor/Interact/Discussions/View_Discussion_Performance.

Blackboard. 2019. "SafeAssign". Accessed January 21, 2019. www.blackboard.com/safeassign/index.html.

Boss, Richard W. 1991. "What Is an Expert System? ERIC Digest." *ERIC Clearinghouse on Information Resources, Syracuse, NY.* July 1991. https://eric.ed.gov/?id=ED335058.

Buchan, Tonya. 2018. "Accelerating Adoption of Adaptive Courseware at Public Universities: Georgia State University Update, Spring 2018." Association of Public and Land-Grant Universities Personalized Learning Consortium. Last Modified May 2018. Accessed February 5, 2019. www.aplu.org/library/2018-colorado-state-university-adaptive-courseware-report/file.

Caliskan, Aylin, Joanna J. Bryson, and Arvind Narayanan. "Semantics Derived Automatically from Language Corpora Contain Human-Like Biases." *Science* 356 no. 6334 (2017): 183–186. doi:10.1126/science.aal4230.

Carter, Don. 2018. "Accelerating Adoption of Adaptive Courseware at Public Universities: Northern Arizona University Update, Spring 2018." Association of Public and Land-Grant Universities Personalized Learning Consortium. Last Modified May 2018. Accessed February 5, 2019. www.aplu.org/library/2018-northern-arizona-university-adaptive-courseware-report/file.

Coast, Ernestina. 2016. "Case Study: Improving Students' Assessment Literacy Using Turnitin Originality Self-Check." LSE Learning Technology and Innovation Case Studies. Last Modified 2016. Accessed January 21, 2019. http://lti.lse.ac.uk/case-study-improving-assessment-literacy-using-tii-originality-self-check/.

Dastin, Jeffrey. 2018. "Amazon Scraps Secret AI Recruiting Tool That Showed Bias Against Women." *Reuters.* October 9, 2018. Accessed February 5, 2019. www.reuters.com/article/us-amazon-com-jobs-automation-insight/amazon-scraps-secret-ai-recruiting-tool-that-showed-bias-against-women-idUSKCN1MK08G.

De Gruyter, Johannes and Kevin Berg. 2018. "Accelerating Adoption of Adaptive Courseware at Public Universities: Portland State University Update, Spring 2018." Association of Public and Land-Grant Universities Personalized Learning Consortium. Last Modified May 2018. Accessed February 5, 2019. www.aplu.org/library/2018-portland-state-university-adaptive-courseware-report/file.

DePaepe, James. 2014. "CWU Teacher Time Study: How Washington Public School Teachers Spend Their Work Days." Central Washington University. Accessed January 21, 2019. www.cwu.edu/teachertimestudy.

EdSurge. *Decoding Adaptive.* London: Pearson, 2016. Accessed February 5, 2019. http://d3e7x39d4i7wbe.cloudfront.net/static_assets/PearsonDecodingAdaptiveWeb.pdf.

EDUCAUSE. 2019. "2019 Key Issues in Teaching and Learning." Last Modified 2019. Accessed February 4, 2019. www.educause.edu/eli/initiatives/key-issues-in-teaching-and-learning.

Evans, Benedict. 2018. "Ways to Think About Machine Learning." Last Modified June 22, 2018. Accessed January 21, 2019. www.ben-evans.com/benedictevans/2018/06/22/ways-to-think-about-machine-learning-8nefy.

Goodwin, Bryan and Kirsten Miller. 2012. "Research Says / Good Feedback is Targeted, Specific, Timely." *Educational Leadership* 70 no. 1 (2012): 82–83. Accessed January 21, 2019. www.ascd.org/publications/educational-leadership/sept12/vol70/num01/Good-Feedback-Is-Targeted,-Specific,-Timely.aspx.

Grammarly. 2019a. "Grammarly Premium." Accessed January 21, 2019. www.grammarly.com/premium.

Grammarly. 2019b. "Grammarly Spotlight: How We Use AI to Enhance Your Writing." Last Modified August 14, 2018. Accessed January 21, 2019. www.grammarly.com/blog/how-grammarly-uses-ai/.

Grammarly. 2019c. "Plagiarism Checker by Grammarly." Accessed January 21, 2019. www.grammarly.com/plagiarism-checker.

Greenwood, Julie. 2018. "Accelerating Adoption of Adaptive Courseware at Public Universities: Oregon State University Update, Spring 2018." Association of Public and Land-Grant Universities Personalized Learning Consortium. Last Modified May 2018. Accessed February 5, 2019. www.aplu.org/library/2018-oregon-state-university-adaptive-courseware-report/file.

Hanke, John. 2018. "A Peek Inside the Niantic Real World Platform." Niantic Blog. Last Modified June 28, 2018. Accessed January 21, 2019. https://nianticlabs.com/blog/nianticrealworldplatform/.

Harlow, Iain M. "Measuring Learning and Potential." *Cerego Insights*. September 26, 2018. Accessed February 5, 2019. https://cdn2.hubspot.net/hubfs/2480790/Cerego%20Insights.pdf.

Harlow, Iain M., Paul T. Mumma, and Andrew Smith Lewis. "Translating Learning Science into Learning Strategy." *Cerego White Paper*. May 1, 2016. Accessed February 5, 2019. https://cerego.com/pdf/Whitepaper.pdf.

Higgins, Richard, Peter Hartley, and Alan Skelton. 2002. "The Conscientious Consumer: reconsidering the role of assessment feedback in student learning." *Studies in Higher Education* 27 no. 1 (2002): 53–64. doi:10.1080/03075070120099368.

Howlin, Colm. "Realizeit System Overview." *Realizeit White Paper*. February 2018. Accessed February 5, 2019. http://realizeitlearning.com/wp-content/uploads/2018/04/System-Overview-Feb-2018.pdf.

Howlin, Colm P. and Danny Lynch. 2014. "A Framework for the Delivery of Personalized Adaptive Content." *In 2014 International Conference on Web and Open Access to Learning (ICWOAL), Dubai, United Arab Emirates*, 25–27 November, 2014. doi:10.1109/ICWOAL.2014.7009203.

Hunt, Jared and Patrick Tompkins. 2014. "A Comparative Analysis of SafeAssign and Turnitin." *Inquiry: The Journal of the Virginia Community Colleges* 19 (2014): 63–73. https://commons.vccs.edu/cgi/viewcontent.cgi?article=1012&context=inquiry.

IBM. 2019. "AI and Bias." IBM Research 5 in 5 Predictions. Accessed February 5, 2019. www.research.ibm.com/5-in-5/ai-and-bias/.

Jenal, Andrin, Nikolay Savinov, Torsten Sattler, and Gaurav Chaurasia. 2019. "RNN-based Generative Model for Fine-Grained Sketching." *arXiv.org Computer Science: Computer Vision and Pattern Recognition*. https://arxiv.org/abs/1901.03991v1.

Johnson, Dale. 2018. "Accelerating Adoption of Adaptive Courseware at Public Universities: Arizona State University Update, Spring 2018." Association of Public and Land-Grant Universities Personalized Learning Consortium. Last Modified May 2018. Accessed February 5, 2019. www.aplu.org/library/2018-arizona-state-university-adaptive-courseware-report/file.

Kahn, Asifullah, Anabia Sohail, Umme Zahoora, and Aqsa Saeed Qureshi. 2019. "A Survey of the Recent Architectures of Deep Convolutional Neural Networks." *arXiv.org Computer Science: Computer Vision and Pattern Recognition*. https://arxiv.org/abs/1901.06032v1.

Laubli, Samuel, Rico Sennrich, and Martin Volk. 2018. "Has Machine Translation Achieved Human Parity? A Case for Document-level Evaluation." *arXiv.org Computer Science: Computation and Language*. https://arxiv.org/abs/1808.07048v1.

Lee, Younggun, Taesu Kim, and Soo-Young Lee. 2018. "Voice Imitating Text-to-Speech Neural Networks." *arXiv.org Computer Science: Sound*. https://arxiv.org/abs/1806.00927v1.

Levin, Sam. 2016. "A Beauty Contest was Judged by AI and the Robots Didn't Like Dark Skin." *The Guardian.* September 8, 2016. Accessed February 5, 2019. www.theguardian.com/technology/2016/sep/08/artificial-intelligence-beauty-contest-doesnt-like-black-people.

Luke, Ryan. 2018. "Accelerating Adoption of Adaptive Courseware at Public Universities: University of Louisville Update, Spring 2018." Association of Public and Land-Grant Universities Personalized Learning Consortium. Last Modified May 2018. Accessed February 5, 2019. www.aplu.org/library/2018-university-of-louisville-adaptive-courseware-report/file.

Lynch, Danny and Colm P. Howlin. 2014. "Real World Usage of an Adaptive Testing Algorithm to Uncover Latent Knowledge." In *7th International Conference of Education, Research, and Innovation, Seville, Spain, 17–19 November, 2014.* ICERI2014 Proceedings: 504–511. IATED. https://lab.realizeitlearning.com/papers/RealWorldUsageUncoverLatentKnowledge.pdf.

McLennan, Sarah, and Mary Gainer. 2012. "When the Computer Wore a Skirt: Langley's Computers, 1935–1970." *NASA Office of Communications History Program Office News and Notes* 29, no. 1 (2012): 25–32.

Miller, Patrick and Xiaojing Duan. 2018. "NGDLE Learning Analytics: Gaining a 360-Degree View of Learning." EDUCAUSE Review Transforming Higher Ed Blog. Last Modified January 30, 2018. Accessed February 4, 2019. https://er.educause.edu/blogs/2018/1/ngdle-learning-analytics-gaining-a-360-degree-view-of-learning.

Mills, Wren. n.d. "Using SafeAssign as a Teaching Tool." Accessed January 21, 2019. www.nyit.edu/ctl/blog/using_safeassign_as_a_teaching_tool.

National Forum on Educational Statistics. *Forum Guide to Early Warning Systems.* U.S. Department of Education. Washington, DC: National Center for Education Statistics, 2018. Accessed February 5, 2019. https://nces.ed.gov/pubs2019/NFES2019035.pdf.

Newton, Derek. 2017. "Want to Be a Better Writer? Try Letting a Robot Tell You What to Do." *Quartz,* June 4, 2017. https://qz.com/997006/how-a-robot-improved-my-writing/.

Nicol, David J. and Debra MacFarlane-Dick. 2006. "Formative Assessment and Self-Regulated Learning: A Model and Seven Principles of Good Feedback Practice." *Studies in Higher Education* 31 (2006): 199–218. doi:10.1080/03075070600572090.

O'Sullivan, Patricia. 2018. "Accelerating Adoption of Adaptive Courseware at Public Universities: University of Mississippi Update, Spring 2018." Association of Public and Land-Grant Universities Personalized Learning Consortium. Last Modified May 2018. Accessed February 5, 2019. www.aplu.org/library/2018-university-of-mississippi-adaptive-courseware-report/file.

Pezdek, Kathy. 2009. "Grading Student Papers: Reducing Faculty Workload While Improving Feedback to Students." *Association for Psychological Science Observer* 22 no. 9 (2009). Accessed January 21, 2019. www.psychologicalscience.org/observer/grading-student-papers-reducing-faculty-workload-while-improving-feedback-to-students.

Sambasivan, Rajiv, Sourish Das, and Sujit K. Sahu. 2018. "A Bayesian Perspective of Statistical Machine Learning for Big Data." *arXiv.org Computer Science: Machine Learning.* https://arxiv.org/abs/1811.04788v2.

Schinske, Jeffrey and Kimberly Tanner. 2014. "Teaching More by Grading Less (or Differently)." *CBE Life Sciences Education* 13 no. 2 (2014): 159–166. doi:10.1187/cbe.cbe-14-03-0054.

Schorn, Susan. 2007. "Parallel Plagiarism Detection Test of TurnItIn, SafeAssign, and Google Preliminary Results." Unpublished results. Accessed January 21, 2019. www.insidehighered.com/sites/default/server_files/files/2007PlagTest.pdf.

Schorn, Susan. 2015. "Replicated Text Detection: Test of TurnItIn." Unpublished results. Accessed January 21, 2019. www.insidehighered.com/sites/default/server_files/files/2015plagtest.pdf.

SmartSparrow. 2018. "What is Adaptive Learning?" Last Modified 2018. Accessed February 5, 2019. www.smartsparrow.com/what-is-adaptive-learning/.

Straumsheim, Carl. 2016. "Detecting More Than Plagiarism." *Inside Higher Ed: News*. Last Modified January 21, 2016. Accessed January 21, 2019. www.insidehighered.com/news/2016/01/21/turnitin-expanding-beyond-plagiarism-detection-launches-revision-assistant.

Tally, Steve. 2009. "Signals Tells Students How They're Doing Even Before the Test." Last Modified September 1, 2009. Accessed February 5, 2019. www.purdue.edu/uns/x/2009b/090827ArnoldSignals.html.

Tesene, Megan. 2018. "Accelerating Adoption of Adaptive Courseware at Public Universities: Georgia State University Update, Spring 2018." Association of Public and Land-Grant Universities Personalized Learning Consortium. Last Modified May 2018. Accessed February 5, 2019. www.aplu.org/library/2018-georgia-state-university-adaptive-courseware-report/file.

Turnitin. 2017. "WriteCheck". Accessed January 21, 2019. http://en.writecheck.com/.

Turnitin. 2019a. "Feedback Studio." Accessed January 21, 2019. www.turnitin.com/products/feedback-studio.

Turnitin. 2019b. "Revision Assistant." Accessed January 21, 2019. www.turnitin.com/products/revision-assistant.

Villasenor, John. 2019. "Artificial Intelligence and Bias: Four Key Challenges." Brookings Techtank. January 3, 2019. Accessed February 5, 2019. www.brookings.edu/blog/techtank/2019/01/03/artificial-intelligence-and-bias-four-key-challenges/.

Vrbanec, Tedo and Ana Mestovic. 2017. "The Struggle with Academic Plagiarism: Approaches Based on Semantic Similarity." In *2017 40th International Convention on Information and Communication Technology, Electronics and Microelectronics (MIPRO), Opatija, Croatia*, May 22–26, 2017, 976–981. IEEE. doi:10.23919/MIPRO.2017.7973544.

Walchuk, Kevin. 2016. "An Examination of the Efficacy of the Plagiariam Detection Software Program Turnitin." Master's thesis, University of Ontario Institute of Technology, 2016.

Wilson, Joanne, Ernesto Pagano, Tyce Henry, and J. Puckett. 2014. "Five Trends to Watch in Higher Education." Last Modified April 10, 2014. www.bcg.com/publications/2014/public-sector-five-trends-watch-higher-education.aspx.

Young, Tom, Devamanyu Hazarika, Soujanya Poria, and Erik Cambria. 2018. "Recent Trends in Deep Learning Based Natural Language Processing." *arXiv.org Computer Science: Computation and Language*. https://arxiv.org/abs/1708.02709v8.

Zerwin, Sarah M. 2011. "How Long Does it Take to Grade 88 Persuasive Research Papers?" The Paper Graders. Last Modified December 13, 2011. Accessed January 21, 2019. http://thepapergraders.org/?p=298.

Index

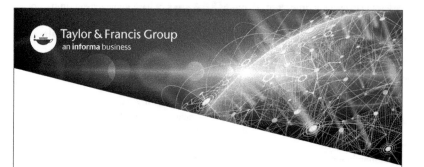

Milton Keynes UK
Ingram Content Group UK Ltd.
UKHW040052071024
449327UK00019B/502